Renewing Your Hope
with the Lord's Prayer

*Learning from Jesus
How to Pray*

Steven Childers
John Frame

"Rare is the book that unveils biblical truth with the depth of a scholar while keeping it accessible for the everyday believer. The challenge is greater when considering such a well-known and beloved passage as the Lord's Prayer. But that is precisely what Steve Childers and John Frame have given us. Wherever you are on your journey with Christ, as you mine these pages you will find the purest ore of truth from God's Word. Read this book, follow its ten steps for each chapter, and then read it again!"

Dr. Ed Stetzer, Dean, Talbot School of Theology at Biola University; regional director for Lausanne North America; author, and writer for USA Today and CNN

"Imagine being invited to one of the best restaurants in the world where two brilliant and seasoned chefs prepare a meal that will change your life. Most of us are not experienced epicures to comprehend the composite glory in the feast. But if we are patiently and kindly taught how each part of the banquet from start to finish reflects our Father in heaven, then the mere delight becomes a transformational covenant meal. Drs. Childers and Frame deliver a feast of hope through an exposition of the Lord's Prayer. It is a tantalizing, soul-filling repass that will change how you taste each word of this life-transforming prayer. Fifty years ago, I sat in Dr. Frame's classes and tasted the richness of his passionate love of Jesus. With his dear friend, Steve Childers, I get to sit at the table and take in the bread of life again. Don't wait—your table is set and waiting for you to dine."

Dr. Dan Allender, Professor of Counseling Psychology and President at The Seattle School of Theology and Psychology; author of *The Wounded Heart, To Be Told*, and *Leading with a Limp*

"Each chapter in *Renewing Your Hope with the Lord's Prayer* by Childers and Frame contains a wonderful combination of (1) a clear explanation of the meaning of a phrase in the Lord's Prayer; (2) a brief but well-informed discussion of certain differences in interpretation found in the academic literature on this phrase; (3) a "whole Bible" perspective on important theological truths implied in each phrase; (4) a section of practical guidance with questions for personal reflection and discussion, a sample prayer, and a list of hymns to encourage worship; and (5) specific recommendations for further study. Readers who work their way through this book will receive the great reward of a deeper prayer life and an enriched personal relationship with God."

Dr. Wayne Grudem, Distinguished Research Professor Emeritus of Theology and Biblical Studies, Phoenix Seminary; author of *Systematic Theology: Introduction to Biblical Doctrine*

"Here is an excellent educational resource for training in theology and practice. In this second volume Childers and Frame use the Lord's Prayer as a framework for teaching and training in the meaning and the practice of prayer. Included are related biblical passages, catechetical questions and answers, and hymns to encourage users to incorporate the insights and practices into their lives."

Dr. Vern Poythress, Distinguished Professor of New

Testament, Biblical Interpretation, and Systematic Theology at Westminster Theological Seminary, Philadelphia

"Renewing Your Hope with the Lord's Prayer is a true gift to God's people. It masterfully weaves rich theological truth with practical application—just as the prayer Jesus taught us does. This book will transform your prayer life in the very way Jesus intended. Read it, and you will not only rise up and call Steve Childers and John Frame blessed for having written it, but, more importantly, you will glorify the God who meets us with his amazing grace and truth."

Dr. Steve Brown, Radio broadcaster, author, former pastor and professor of Practical Theology at Reformed Theological Seminary–Orlando; author of *A Scandalous Freedom*

"I thank God for Steve Childers and John Frame, two of my most beloved seminary professors. Many of my best memories from those days are from their classes—and still today my personal life and public ministry are enriched daily by truths (and triangles!) I learned from them. So, I rejoice greatly that these two long-time colleagues have teamed up again, now to make world-class seminary-level training more available worldwide, especially for leaders in underserved places. Read this alone, and you'll benefit. Gather a group to study together, and you'll supercharge your learning. Glean every precious crumb you can from these two wise, insightful, spiritual, tested, resilient professors!"

Rev. David Mathis, Senior Teacher and Executive Editor, Desiring God Ministries; adjunct professor, Bethlehem College & Seminary, Minneapolis; author of *Habits of Grace*

"This work deserves a prominent place amidst the historic corpus of admirable works on the Lord's Prayer. This is a treasure trove of searching exegesis, expansive historic and theological resources and accessible application. The newest believer and the most seasoned Christian will find heart-deep help here."

Rev. Joe Novenson, Former Senior Teaching Pastor at Lookout Mountain Presbyterian Church (PCA) in Lookout Mountain, Tennessee (1997-2018)

"This is the best teaching resource and guide I've ever seen on the Lord's Prayer. It has been my privilege to teach underserved and under resourced church leaders and pastors in a dozen countries on five continents, and in my experience this book on the Lord's Prayer could not be more perfectly suited for its intended purpose. It is perfectly designed for training and equipping pastors, church leaders, and the members of the body of Christ. It is filled with biblical and theological insight, is immensely practical, and spiritually nourishing. By God's grace, this is a book that teaches, instructs, edifies, corrects, and encourages us to pray as Jesus taught us."

Dr. Steven West, Lead Pastor at Crestwicke Baptist Church in Ontario; adjunct professor at Heritage Seminary (Cambridge) and Toronto Baptist Seminary; writer for The Gospel Coalition.

"Whether in a counseling session or a one-on-one with a college student, the conversation will often shift to the question: How do I pray? The response, "the Lord's Prayer," now comes with a great resource for study. *Renewing Your Hope with the Lord's Prayer* provides both robust theology and practical step-by-step guided study applied so the reader really understands the purpose and hope of Jesus's words about prayer. The authors show how to use this book for the desired outcomes of instilling the desire for life-long learning and growth in the practice of prayer, whatever one's stage in life or circumstances."

Rev. **Rod Mays**, Board Chair, Christian Counseling and Educational Foundation; Coordinator Emeritus, Reformed University Fellowship; adjunct faculty, Reformed Theological Seminary

"Something as wonderful, widely known, and spiritually powerful as the Lord's Prayer deserves to be treasured, savored, and shared. Drs. Childers and Frame have offered us a work uniquely valuable toward that end in their book, *Renewing Your Hope with the Lord's Prayer*. They bring their rare and much-needed combination of biblical, theological, and pastoral depth to this work in such a way that every reader is both enriched spiritually and equipped for ministry. Every phrase in the prayer is examined with a depth of detail rarely found in a book so accessible and engaging. And yet the hope-filled heart of the prayer is very much kept alive as its riches are brought to light."

Rev. **Larry Kirk**, Pastor Emeritus at Christ Community Church (Evangelical Free Church) in Daytona Beach, Florida; adjunct professor of Pastoral Theology, Reformed Theological Seminary

"In *Renewing Your Hope with the Lord's Prayer*, Steve Childers and John Frame offer a theologically robust tool to spur all sorts of people in all sorts of contexts towards love and good deeds. The flexibility of how this resource can be used individually, in groups, in pastoral training, and in missions is one its best features. Rich in biblical fidelity, historical rootedness, and practical application, this resource in this excellent series will surely benefit Jesus' church and advance his Kingdom."

Rev. **Brian Salter**, Lead Pastor, Lookout Mountain Presbyterian Church, Lookout Mountain, Tennessee; former staff with Cru in East Asia and the University of Georgia campus

"*Renewing Your Hope with the Lord's Prayer* is a theologically rich and practically transformative study that takes one of Jesus' most familiar teachings and reveals its profound implications for all of life. Rooted in Reformed theology and historic Christian orthodoxy, this book demonstrates that the Lord's Prayer is not just a model but the foundation for all Christian prayer—shaping our communion with God according to our ultimate purpose: to glorify Him and enjoy Him forever. This study informs the mind with biblical truth, stirs the heart to worship with deep spiritual affections, and fosters real growth in the practice of prayer. Designed for adult learning, it equips believers to pray with greater depth, conviction, and joy—aligning all our prayers with the certainty of our hope in God's glory through Jesus Christ. If you long to grow in fellowship with God through prayer, I highly recommend this study. Biblically rich and practically powerful, it is a valuable resource for both individual use and corporate study within the church."

Rev. Kenny Stokes, Pastor, Bethlehem Baptist Church; Associate Professor for Church Planting, Bethlehem College and Seminary, Minneapolis, Minnesota

"Biblical hope is grounded in confident trust in our sovereign Father. This study of the Lord's Prayer will help you pray with hope but also live with hope and even sing with hope."

Dr. Robert C. (Ric) Cannada, Jr., Chancellor Emeritus and Associate Professor of Practical Theology Emeritus at Reformed Theological Seminary

"*Renewing Your Hope with the Lord's Prayer* combines strong scholarship, crystal clear writing, sound exegesis, effective learning strategies, and penetrating application to help readers strengthen their hope by learning to pray the Lord's Prayer with deepened understanding and confidence that the Father's kingdom will come and his will will be done globally, in the consummated, glorious kingdom that is the fulfillment of God's original plan for this world."

Dr. John. J. Hughes, Director of Academic Development and Academic Project Manager, P&R Publishing; author and editor of *The Classic Warfield Collection*

"I know of no other books than the Applied Theology series that better display the power of the gospel, the profundity of centuries of theological insight, and the simplicity of master teachers. *Renewing Your Hope with the Lord's Prayer* is a book that church and school leaders around the world should read first to kindle their own prayer life and then read again with their class or small group to share the hope of the world."

Prof. Ravi Jain, Asst. Professor of Liberal Studies, Eastern University; co-author of *The Liberal Arts Tradition: A Philosophy of Christian Classical Education* (Third Edition)

What People are Saying About The Applied Theology Series

"After fifty years of seminary teaching John Frame has much wisdom to impart. And it is always a good thing when we can listen to his voice again. Teamed up with Steve Childers with his decades of pastoring and teaching, we get a mature and seasoned theology that is for the sake of the church. And that is the way it should always be. The Applied Theology Series is simply written and clear, and full of nourishing insight for pastors today. Pathway Learning is fulfilling an important need in making theological education accessible to churches that need it. It is rooted in a gospel as wide as creation, there are various educational approaches that really aid pastors in ministry, and it is culturally sensitive to varied contexts. May the Lord bless this endeavor."

Dr. Michael Goheen, Professor of Missional Theology, Calvin Theological Seminary; Director of Theological Education, Missional Training Center, Phoenix

"Thanks to the efforts of John Frame and Steve Childers, The Applied Theology series offers a unique resource for people eager to grow in biblical knowledge and godly practice. They are trying to hold theology and application together, which makes it relevant for all Christian readers. Drawing from both a systematic and a practical theologian—each with deep training and decades of teaching experience—readers will benefit from a product that is accessible, useful, and life-giving. May many profit greatly from these efforts."

Dr. Kelly Kapic, Professor of Theological Studies, Covenant College; author of *You're Only Human: How Your Limits Reflect God's Design and Why That's Good News*

"Sadly, the modern church has lost its vital connection between theology and Christian experience. A thriving faith requires both spiritual depth and intellectual engagement. In this series, John Frame and Steve Childers have bridged this gap. Frame has devoted his whole life to theology, while Childers brings deep pastoral wisdom from his decades as a ministry practitioner and professor. Together they have created a series of books and courses for which we owe them a debt. I heartily encourage readers to utilize these helpful resources."

Dr. John H. Armstrong, Author, former pastor in Reformed Church in America; adjunct professor, Wheaton College Graduate School

This book is dedicated to the millions of gifted and called church leaders without access to the training and tools they need to plant and grow healthy churches that transform lives and communities.

"What a great pity that the prayer of such a master is prattled and chattered so irreverently all over the world! ... In a word, the Lord's Prayer is the greatest martyr on earth.... Everybody tortures and abuses it; few take comfort and joy in its proper use."

–Martin Luther

CONTENTS

READ THIS FIRST

Most books are written to be read.
Pathway Learning books are written **to be walked.**

Each chapter is a guided learning path with ten carefully designed steps that help you move beyond merely understanding biblical truth to experiencing its power to change your life. One of those ten steps is the familiar "Read the Chapter article"—the same kind of content you'd expect in any traditional book. But the other nine steps are where real transformation begins.

Before and after your reading step, you'll find steps that help you prepare your heart, reflect deeply, apply Scripture to real-life situations, and engage in prayer, worship, and practical action. Some steps are meant for personal reflection—but most are intentionally designed to be taken with others. That's because God designed his image bearers to learn best in authentic, loving community.

Try taking these steps alone and you'll quickly see why! (It's hard to have a rich discussion about how someone else is applying these truths if that "someone else" doesn't exist.) So don't just read this book—walk its paths together with a friend, mentor, or small group. When you do, you'll discover how God uses this process to renew your mind, stir your heart, and shape your life to be more like Christ.

ABOUT THE AUTHORS

Steven L. Childers

Dr. Steve Childers is the founder and president of Pathway Learning with the mission to help underserved church leaders plant and grow healthy churches that transform lives and communities around the world. For twenty-two years, he served as a resident professor of practical theology at Reformed Theological Seminary in Orlando, teaching evangelism, discipleship (spiritual formation), church planting, church renewal, missions, and leadership.

Before being a professor, Steve planted and pastored two churches—urban and suburban—for fifteen years as an ordained minister in the Presbyterian Church in America. He has helped train thousands of church leaders around the world by using his church leadership training curriculum, translated in several languages. He is a graduate of Covenant Theological Seminary in St. Louis, Trinity Evangelical Divinity School in Chicago, and Reformed Theological Seminary in Orlando. He has also studied global missions and leadership at Fuller Theological Seminary in Los Angeles. Steve and his wife, Becky, live in Chattanooga, Tennessee, and have three adult daughters and four grandchildren.

John M. Frame

Dr. John Frame served as a seminary professor of systematic theology and philosophy for almost fifty years. His areas of specialty are systematic theology, apologetics, ethics, and philosophy. John began his teaching career in 1968 on the faculty of Westminster Theological Seminary in Philadelphia. He later served as a founding faculty member at Westminster Seminary California. In 2002, he began teaching at Reformed Theological Seminary in Orlando, and retired in 2017. He now works with Pathway Learning and Steve Childers as coauthor and theological editor of the Applied Theology Project. He's best known for his prolific writings, particularly his four-volume Theology of Lordship series.

John is a graduate of Princeton University, Westminster Theological Seminary, and Yale University, as well as an ordained minister in the Presbyterian Church in America. He is deeply committed to the work of ministry and to training church planters, pastors, and missionaries. Students appreciate his wealth of insight and his ability to communicate complex issues simply and clearly. Students also value John's practical definition of *theology* as "the application of God's revelation to all of life." He is a talented pianist and organist as well as a discerning media critic. He and his late wife, Mary, have five children: Debbie, Doreen, Skip, Justin, and Johnny.

ALSO BY THE AUTHORS

APPLIED THEOLOGY I COLLECTION
Introduction to Theology Trilogy
Essentials in Theology

Foundations in Theology

Perspectives in Theology

APPLIED THEOLOGY II COLLECTION
Faith, Hope, and Love Trilogy
Renewing Your Faith with the Apostles' Creed

Renewing Your Hope with the Lord's Prayer

Renewing Your Love with the Ten Commandments

ACKNOWLEDGMENTS

We are deeply grateful to our Pathway Learning partners in the gospel who want to see the world become a better place by being saturated with healthy churches through which people and societies flourish. Through their sacrificial prayers and gifts, they are helping underserved church leaders around the world receive the high-quality, seminary-level education they need to develop churches with effective ministries of evangelism, discipleship, and mercy.

SERIES PREFACE

After serving on the faculty of three theological institutions for forty-nine years, I retired from teaching in May 2017.[1] It did occur to me that one more year would have brought me to my fiftieth year—not only a round number, but, in biblical terms, a Jubilee. So I was somewhat on the alert for a future teaching ministry that God might open up to me that I could accomplish in that magical fiftieth year.

As it turned out, God did open to me a Jubilee project with Pathway Learning in this Applied Theology series.[2] Typically (for that is the way God works), he had been preparing it through eternal ages, but, in our human lifetimes, for decades. When I first came to Reformed Theological Seminary in 2000, I encountered many colleagues with whom I had had long rela-

---

1. Westminster Theological Seminary in Philadelphia, Westminster Seminary California, and Reformed Theological Seminary, Orlando.

2. For Old Testament Israel, the Jubilee (יובל) is the year at the end of seven cycles of sabbatical years. It's sometimes referred to as the Sabbath's Sabbath. There is some debate whether it was the forty-ninth year, the last of seven sabbatical cycles, or whether it was the following fiftieth year. So there is a biblical argument that John may have reached his Jubilee (Steve).

tionships. Seven members of the RTS faculty had been former students of mine. Then there were others who had read books of mine and found my teachings helpful.

One of those was Steve Childers, an experienced pastor and church planter who was now a professor of Practical Theology at RTS, as well as a trainer of church planters and missionaries around the world. When we chatted at the door before my first faculty meeting, Steve told me that he was trying to reconstruct all the RTS practical theology courses to make them triperspectival and to show the students that the best practical theology was an application of biblical doctrine.[3]

Steve and I became not only colleagues but good friends, with offices next door to each other for the next seventeen years. Steve told me how much my article "Proposal for a New Seminary," written almost fifty years ago, had impacted his thinking about the need to educate church leaders without removing them from their local churches and communities.[4]

In 2001, I wrote a postscript to the article in which I looked back on the nearly thirty years of seminary education that had elapsed since I wrote it. The article had not been widely acclaimed, but it had generated enough interest for me to remark occasionally, without any seriousness at all, that it had a "cult following." In that postscript, I lauded some of the advances I'd seen in seminary education during the previous thirty years. I wrote about how it was fun for me to reread what I had been saying when I was younger, bolder, and more radical.

I've mellowed somewhat since that time, but my heart still

---

3. You will learn about this buzzword, *triperspectival*, and many others as you peruse our Applied Theology series. Another emphasis of mine (John) has been to define *"theology"* as "the application of the Word of God by persons to all areas of life," and that definition lies behind the title of our current series.
4. "Proposal for a New Seminary," https://frame-poythress.org/proposal-for-a-new-seminary/.

was, and is, in that Proposal, as reflected in my final words of the postscript:

> The economics of theological training is a subject that needs to be explored in this context. I am not the one to do it. But is there some way that the people of God can be moved by a vision for theological education, as they are often moved by appeals for support of missions? Something like that would have to happen if churches are to become seminaries in the spirit of my Proposal.
>
> Even after much progress in theological education, most church leader training, at home and abroad, is still based on the academic, university model for training scholars rather than practitioners. And the options are often still the same: 1) biblical and theological training without the practical, or 2) practical training without the biblical and theological. Most church leaders still receive their education primarily in residential class-rooms and conference seminars without being mentored theologically and practically, including in their spiritual lives, as they serve in their local churches and communities.

In 2016, during my last academic year of teaching, Steve shared with me a new vision for theological education, called Pathway Learning, to provide underserved church leaders with access to affordable, practical, seminary-level courses where they live, in their language, and adapted to their culture. For years I've been teaching that "theology is application." Steve's challenge was for the two of us to finish our races well, I as a systematic theologian and he as a practical theologian, by collaborating and converging our decades of teaching and ministry "for the nations," as his email signature often says.

The Applied Theology series was born out of this vision to

use the latest advances in educational technology to help bring all the topics of systematic theology to the millions of church leaders, especially in the developing world, who have no access to or cannot afford high-quality traditional seminary education. So our writing began in weekly meetings in our offices that fall, as we discussed the entire body of systematic theology week in and week out, seeking to apply it to all of life and ministry.

Applied Theology is a very intentional, missional, and practical approach to all the traditional topics of systematic theology. As such, it engages everything we are. Not only is it an intellectual accumulation of information, but it involves our head, heart, and hands for the sake of Christ and his kingdom. My hope and prayer is that God will use our collaboration in Applied Theology to help his people apply God's Word to all areas of their lives, for the sake of the nations and the honor of Jesus Christ.

Dr. John M. Frame
Emeritus Professor of Systematic Theology and Philosophy,
Reformed Theological Seminary

PREFACE

Apart from Jesus and the apostle Paul, no one has shaped Christianity more than Augustine (354–430). Near the end of his life, when asked to summarize the essence of biblical Christianity, Augustine pointed to Paul's three virtues of faith, hope, and love in 1 Corinthians 13:13 and linked them to the Apostles' Creed, the Lord's Prayer, and the Ten Commandments.

This ancient trilogy became a simple framework for the formation of what Christians believe (the Apostles' Creed), where they place their hope (the Lord's Prayer), and how they love (the Ten Commandments). It became the foundation for the education of clergy throughout the Middle Ages and was later adopted by the Protestant Reformers, including Martin Luther and John Calvin, and embedded in the great confessions—playing a major role in shaping the Western church.

This framework became widely influential because of its simplicity and accessibility. Even those who could not read could memorize the Apostles' Creed, the Lord's Prayer, and the Ten Commandments, allowing these core truths to be integrated into weekly worship and embedded deeply into their lives—strengthening their faith, hope, and love.

However, despite its powerful legacy, this ancient pattern has been largely lost in the modern church. The once widely known and practiced trilogy that formed the foundation of Christian life and worship is now mostly forgotten.

To help recover this lost framework, we are writing the Faith, Hope, and Love Trilogy as part of this Applied Theology book collection—which includes books on renewing your faith with the Apostles' Creed, renewing your hope with the Lord's Prayer, and renewing your love with the Ten Commandments.

Our goal is not only the renewal of minds, but also the renewal of heart affections that result in transformed lives marked by greater conformity to the image of Jesus Christ.

This present volume is about hope and will explain it by expounding the Lord's Prayer (Matt. 6:9–13; Luke 11:2–4). In Scripture, hope is not a temperamental optimism, nor is it a scientific process of analyzing our circumstances, weighing the chance of positive against the chance of negative ones. Rather, it is a sure and certain trust that all will be well, grounded in God's own sure revelation.

Such a hope leads us to pray, not because we fear that God will not keep his word, but because we are sure that he will. That confidence authorizes us to pray, knowing that our prayer will be effective, knowing that God fully intends to answer us favorably.

So our hope is based on a conviction from Scripture that our future is governed by a loving heavenly Father who will certainly provide for us, his family, forgive our iniquities, and heal all our infirmities. The Lord's Prayer identifies God as precisely that kind of Father, glorious in his heavenly Being and in his holy name. In prayer, we trust that his kingdom will certainly come and bring to our world universal obedience to his will.

The power and love of this great Father will meet all our needs, most amazingly the need we have for forgiveness of our sins against him. And he not only forgives us; he gives us new hearts, that we may forgive others as he has forgiven us.

To be sure, there is evil in the world until the final judgment, but our Father gives us victory over it, and one day that victory will be visible: all will see the triumph of God's kingdom in power and glory, forever.

This is the biblical theology of hope. Over the past fifty years or so, theologians have discussed a different "theology of hope," in which hope is linked to uncertainty rather than certainty. But like so many other modern theological ideas, this view turns everything upside down.

The biblical theology of hope is based on certainty—not the certainty of temperamental optimism or of scientific rationalism, but the comforting words of our Father in heaven, found in his sure Word to us.

Dr. Steven L. Childers
Dr. John M. Frame

INTRODUCTION: LEARNING PATHS

This book will help guide you in developing a steadfast hope in your life that is grounded in the life-changing truths that Jesus taught in the Lord's Prayer. The focus is on helping you apply these biblical truths to your daily life and ministry in a way that helps you to know, love, and serve God as the triune Lord in every area of your life.

Goals

In this book, you'll be equipped to:

- Understand the setting, meaning, and purpose of the Lord's Prayer.
- Learn how to ask our Father in heaven to honor his name.
- Pray for God's kingdom and will to come on earth as it is in heaven.
- Petition God for our daily needs, protection, and obedience in faith.

- Ask God to forgive our sins as we forgive those who sin against us.
- Request God not to lead us into temptation but to deliver us from evil.

Outcomes

Clearly defined, measurable outcomes will help you track your progress toward your learning goals (above). While helpful for self-assessment, these outcomes become even more effective with a qualified mentor, coach, or facilitator who provides you with valuable feedback, accountability, and deeper insights to enhance your personal growth in knowledge, character, and skills.

- I know the context of the Lord's Prayer and its intended purpose for Jesus' disciples.
- I grasp the communal nature of faith reflected in praying to God as our Father and how to pray for God's name to be set apart and honored in prayer.
- I understand how to ask God to glorify his name by causing his kingdom to come and for God's will to be done on earth as it is in heaven.
- I know how to pray for God's daily provision for all things we need for life and for our daily protection, trusting in the Father's care.
- I know what it means to pray for God's ongoing forgiveness of our sins as we forgive others.
- I know why and how I need to ask our Father not to lead us into temptation and what it means to ask our Father to keep delivering us from evil.

Pathway Learning Steps

All Pathway Learning book chapters are uniquely designed with ten innovative learning steps that guide you through a transformational process, far beyond simply reading and acquiring new information, to help you achieve each chapter's goals and outcomes. While most traditional books offer only a chapter to read—which seldom results in lasting life change—Pathway Learning books include the same full chapter content, but reading it is just one of ten learning steps, called "Read the Chapter Article."

The remaining learning steps in each chapter, both before and after the chapter article, show how the biblical truths can be practically applied to your life and ministry, leading to holistic transformation. This innovative learning process, known as Pathway Learning, engages your mind, heart, and behaviors. And with the guidance of a qualified mentor, coach, or facilitator, it leads to lasting transformation in your life and ministry.

Each book chapter includes these ten learning steps:

STEP ONE: Read the Introduction

The Introduction provides a summary of the content covered in each chapter. It serves as a roadmap, helping you recall what has been learned and what lies ahead. Refer to the Introduction as you progress through the book to stay on track with the chapter's key themes.

STEP TWO: Review the Learning Goals

Each chapter's Learning Goals outline the knowledge, character, and skills you will seek to develop as you complete all the learning steps. They are designed to help you focus on the chapter's overall purpose. Reviewing these goals before engaging with the material will enable you to approach each chapter with a clear understanding of what you are aiming to learn and apply.

STEP THREE: Review the Key Ideas

The Key Ideas highlight the desired major takeaways of each chapter. These ideas summarize the essential truths you need to understand and apply. Use them to prepare for the chapter and to review previous chapters, reinforcing your grasp of the overall content.

STEP FOUR: Answer the Reflection Questions

The Reflection Questions are designed to help you connect your personal beliefs, desires, and practices with the topics that you're about to study. This helps motivate you in your upcoming process of learning.

STEP FIVE: Read the Chapter Article with Academic Notes

This step involves the reading of the traditional book chapter, which contains the foundational biblical and theological content that you read in your completion of the first four learning steps. The Academic Notes are provided as chapter footnotes for readers seeking a more in-depth, seminary-level engagement with the chapter's key concepts.

STEP SIX: Answer the Review Questions with Answer Key

The Review Questions are designed to help you recall and reinforce the key concepts from the chapter article. Although the Answer Key is available and helpful, try to answer the questions independently first. This will test your understanding and retention, ensuring that the foundational truths of each chapter are fully grasped.

STEP SEVEN: Answer the Discussion Questions with Sample Answers

The Discussion Questions are intended to deepen your understanding, awaken your heart's desires, and nurture your love for God and others. You can explore them individually or in a group setting. To encourage deeper reflection, try engaging with the questions on your own before consulting the provided sample answers in the Answer Key.

STEP EIGHT: Take the Review Quiz with Answer Key

The Review Quiz helps reinforce the key points of each chapter, aiding in recalling and applying what you've learned. Completing the quiz at the end of the chapter—or before starting the next—will strengthen your understanding. As with other steps, try answering the questions on your own first before reviewing the answers provided in the Answer Key to enhance your learning experience.

STEP NINE: Meditate and Pray

This step invites you to pause and reflect on what God is teaching you in the chapter, allowing these truths to stir your heart to worship him for who he is and what he does. Conclude each chapter with prayer and worship, using the model of adoration, confession, thanksgiving, and supplication. Afterward, consider recording any new insights for practical application to your life and ministry.

In this book, each chapter includes sample prayers based

on the individual petitions of the Lord's Prayer. These examples have been thoughtfully crafted to guide you in praying through the Lord's Prayer during personal devotions, with your family, in small groups, and within your local church.

STEP TEN: Go Deeper as a Lifelong Learner (with Resources)

This step encourages your deeper exploration by using key resources drawn from the chapter article and its academic notes to help you grow in your understanding and application of biblical truths, promoting your lifelong learning and continued growth in spiritual maturity.

Study Schedules

The following table suggests four plans for working through the *Renewing Your Hope with the Lord's Prayer* course and this companion book. Whether you are going through this course or book on your own or with a cohort group, these schedules should help you plan the next steps on your learning pathway.

Week	Extended 12-Week Plan	Standard 8-Week Plan	Abbreviated 6-Week Plan	Intensive 4-Week Plan
	Lesson	Lesson	Lesson	Lesson
1	Intro & 1a	Intro	Intro & 1	Intro & 1
2	1b	1	2	2 & 3
3	2a	2	3	4 & 5
4	2b	3	4	6 & Concl
5	3a	4	5	
6	3b	5	6 & Concl	
7	4a	6		
8	4b	Concl		
9	5a			
10	5b			
11	6a			
12	6b & Concl			

GODWARD PETITIONS

1

OUR HOPE

Step One: Read the Introduction

The Lord's Prayer is the way that Jesus taught his disciples to pray and the way that most Christians have prayed throughout history, including those among the Orthodox, Catholic, and Protestant traditions.

The New Testament reveals two accounts of Jesus' teaching his disciples this prayer. In Matthew's account, Jesus' primary focus is on people's underlying motivations for prayer—his followers are to have the motivation of dearly beloved children who long to know and honor God as their heavenly Father, by praying to God as "our Father." In Luke's account, Jesus is teaching his disciples to be persistent in their prayers, first and foremost for the Father's name to be honored, for his kingdom to come, and for his will to be done on earth as it is in heaven.

The petitions in the Lord's Prayer are divided into two categories: (1) Godward petitions focusing on God's honor, and (2) manward petitions focusing on human needs. The Godward and manward petitions should be seen as a whole. Augustine teaches that in the Godward petitions we "ask for eternal goods" and that in the manward petitions we "ask for temporal goods, which are, however, necessary for obtaining the eternal goods."[1]

Jesus teaches us to follow this model in all our prayers so that we will understand that our purpose in life is the same as his—to hallow the Father's name by causing his kingdom to come and his will to be done on earth as it is in heaven. He wants us not only to believe these truths with our minds but to embrace them in prayer with our heart affections so that we will live out our whole lives in light of them.

In this chapter, you will learn to understand the setting, meaning, and purpose of the Lord's Prayer.

Step Two: Review the Learning Goals

Learning Goals

In this chapter, you will be equipped to:

- Recognize the setting of the Lord's Prayer in Matthew's account and Luke's account.
- Identify and see the relationship between the two categories of Godward and manward petitions.
- Explain how the Lord's Prayer is the hope of the gospel in life.

Step Three: Review the Key Ideas

Key Ideas

In this chapter, these are the key ideas:

- Matthew portrays Jesus as focusing on our

---

1. Augustine, *The Enchiridion on Faith, Hope, and Love*, trans. J. F. Shaw (Dutton, 1955), 30.

underlying motivations for prayer while Luke portrays Jesus as focusing on the importance of persisting in our prayers.

- Godward petitions focus on God's honor. Manward petitions focus on our needs and are the means for the fulfillment of our Godward petitions.
- We follow this model prayer to learn that our purpose in life is the same as Jesus' and to kindle the hope of the gospel in our hearts and lives.

Step Four: Answer the Reflection Questions

Take a moment before reading the chapter article to reflect on these questions. They'll help you connect your beliefs, desires, and practices with the topics ahead, allowing for deeper engagement and more practical application to your life and ministry.

1. Do you regularly pray the Lord's Prayer? If so, how do you pray it?
2. How do you think the petitions in the Lord's Prayer relate to one another?

Step Five: Read the Chapter Article with Academic Notes

The Apostles' Creed, the Lord's Prayer, and the Ten Commandments summarize the essence of what followers of Christ believe, why they have hope, and how they should live.

The Lord's Prayer is the way that Jesus taught his disciples to pray and the way that most Christians have prayed throughout history, including those among the Orthodox, Roman Catholic, and Protestant traditions.[2]

---

2. Besides the New Testament, the earliest summary of Christian beliefs and

The New Testament reveals two accounts of Jesus' teaching his disciples this prayer. The first account is early in his ministry, probably in Galilee, when he gives the Sermon on the Mount (Matt. 6:9–13). The second account is later in his ministry, probably in Judea, when one of his disciples asks him to teach them how to pray (Luke 11:2–4). Jesus gives us this prayer in five simple verses in the Matthew 6 account:

> Pray then like this:
>> Our Father in heaven,
>> hallowed be your name.
>> Your kingdom come,
>> your will be done,
>> on earth as it is in heaven.
>> Give us this day our daily bread,
>> and forgive us our debts,
>> as we also have forgiven our debtors.
>> And lead us not into temptation,
>> but deliver us from evil.[3] [For yours is the kingdom and the
> power and the glory, forever. Amen.][4]

---

practices is found in a first-century document called the *Didache*, from the Greek word Διδαχή, "Teaching." It includes a list of beliefs, including the Ten Commandments and the Lord's Prayer, that were taught to converts before they were baptized.

3. We'll study later how the formatting of these verses reflects the relationship between the prayer's primary and supporting petitions, e.g., God's kingdom comes *when* his will is done on earth as it is in heaven, we ask the Father to forgive us our debts *as we* also have forgiven our debtors, and our temptation includes the *evil* from which we need deliverance.

4. The traditional doxology is found in the majority of New Testament Greek manuscripts (Textus Receptus and Majority Text), including the Greek uncials dating from the fifth to the tenth centuries and the Greek minuscules dating from the ninth to the twelfth centuries. This is why the doxology is included in the English KJV and NKJV versions. But the doxology is not found in the earlier and best Greek manuscripts, including א, B, D, f1, various Latin and Coptic versions, and numerous church fathers. It's also not found in Luke's account of the Lord's Prayer in Luke 11:2–4. So most modern English Bible translations

Jesus' intention in teaching his disciples to pray in this new way is so that they would begin to think, hope, and live in a new way. He knew that it was not possible for them to pray like this without aligning their lives with their prayers. So the Lord's Prayer is marvelously full of meaning.[5] Theologian J. I. Packer observes that the Lord's Prayer is "a key to the whole business of living. What it means to be a Christian is nowhere clearer than here."[6]

THE SETTING of the Prayer

Before examining the individual petitions in this prayer, it can be helpful to understand the contexts in which Jesus taught it in Matthew and Luke.

In Matthew's account, Jesus teaches this prayer in the middle of his warning against the dangers of practicing reli-

---

either do not include it or place it in a margin or footnote, e.g., RSV and NIV. The use of this doxology probably arose when the prayer began to be used in public worship and needed a doxology at the end. It may be based on 1 Chronicles 29:11, "Yours, O LORD, is the greatness and the power and the glory and the victory and the majesty, for all that is in the heavens and in the earth is yours. Yours is the kingdom, O LORD and you are exalted as head above all." So it's fine for believers to use this doxology to conclude the prayer, but it should not be seen as belonging to Jesus' teaching.

5. The Anglican Prayer Book Catechism reveals the fuller meaning of the Lord's Prayer. Question: "What desirest thou of God in this prayer?" Answer: "I desire my Lord God our heavenly Father, who is the giver of all goodness, to send his grace unto me, and to all people, that we may worship him, serve him, and obey him, as we ought to do. And I pray unto God, that he will send us all things that be needful both for our souls and bodies; and that he will be merciful unto us, and forgive us our sins; and that it will please him to save and defend us in all dangers ghostly [i.e., spiritual] and bodily; and that he will keep us from all sin and wickedness, and from our ghostly enemy, and from everlasting death. And this I trust he will do of his mercy and goodness, through our Lord Jesus Christ. And therefore I say, Amen. So be it."

6. The early church father Tertullian refers to the Lord's Prayer as "a compendium of the gospel." The English Puritan Thomas Watson calls it "a body of divinity." J. I. Packer, *Growing in Christ* (Crossway, 1994).

gious righteousness to be approved by people. He begins this part of his Sermon on the Mount by saying, "Beware of practicing your righteousness before other people in order to be seen by them" (Matt. 6:1).

Then Jesus uses the common practices of giving, praying, and fasting to help his hearers understand how they should practice these spiritual disciplines. In each of these three examples, Jesus draws a stark contrast between how religious hypocrites practice righteousness and how his followers should practice it. When he addresses the practice of prayer, he distinguishes his approach to prayer with the religious traditions and practices in his day:

> And when you pray, you must not be like the hypocrites. For they love to stand and pray in the synagogues and at the street corners, that they may be seen by others....
>
> And when you pray, do not heap up empty phrases as the Gentiles do, for they think that they will be heard for their many words. Do not be like them. (Matt. 6:5–8)

Jesus' primary focus is on people's underlying motivations for prayer. The pagans and religious hypocrites pray to earn favor with their audience or God by calling attention to themselves. Jesus warns, "Do not be like them." Instead, Jesus teaches his followers to have the motivation of dearly beloved children who long to know and honor God as their heavenly Father, by praying to God as "our Father."

In Luke's account, Jesus teaches this prayer in response to a request from one of his disciples to teach them how to pray, soon after they observed Jesus finish his prayers. Luke writes, "Now Jesus was praying in a certain place, and when he finished, one of his disciples said to him, 'Lord, teach us to pray, as John taught his disciples'" (Luke 11:1).

The disciples regularly observed Jesus' practice of prayer,

including times when he would secretly separate himself from them to pray. Mark tells us, "Rising very early in the morning, while it was still dark, he departed and went out to a desolate place, and there he prayed" (Mark 1:35). Many times, the disciples also heard Jesus pray when he was with them. There was something unique and compelling about how Jesus prayed that made his disciples want to learn how to pray like him.[7]

Luke's account of Jesus' teaching this prayer in Luke 11:2–4 is immediately followed by his account of Jesus' continuing to teach about prayer in Luke 11:5–13. So what does Jesus teach his disciples about how to pray after giving them the Lord's Prayer?

In Luke 11:5–13, Jesus teaches his disciples to keep praying to God as their Father with the persistent, shameless boldness of dearly beloved children. To illustrate this, he tells his disciples a parable about a man who has a need and knocks persistently on his friend's door late at night until he finally gets up from his bed to answer (Luke 11:5–8). Then Jesus says:

> I tell you, ask, and it will be given to you; seek, and you will find; knock, and it will be opened to you. For everyone who asks receives, and the one who seeks finds, and to the one who knocks it will be opened. What father among you, if his son asks for a fish, will instead of a fish give him a serpent; or if he asks for an egg, will give him a scorpion? (Luke 11:9–12)

Jesus is teaching his disciples to be persistent in praying in the way he had just taught them to pray—to be persistent in their prayers first and foremost for the Father's name to be

---

7. It seems likely that when Jesus prayed, he used the same model for prayer that he taught his disciples in the "Lord's Prayer." This argues against those who advocate changing the name of this prayer to the "Disciples' Prayer."

honored, for his kingdom to come, and for his will to be done on earth as it is in heaven.

Jesus ends his teaching on how to pray by promising his disciples that the Father will answer their persistent prayers by giving them the greatest gift they could ever ask for as his children—the gift of himself in the Holy Spirit. Jesus assures them, "If you then, who are evil, know how to give good gifts to your children, how much more will the heavenly Father give the Holy Spirit to those who ask him!" (Luke 11:13).

Jesus is teaching that God himself is the ultimate gift to all those who "keep asking, seeking, and knocking" in their prayers. The greatest answer to prayer is not receiving what we ask God to give us—even things like our daily bread, forgiveness, and deliverance from temptation and evil—but the far superior gift of knowing, loving, and honoring the Giver as our Father in heaven.

THE MEANING of the Prayer

The Lord's Prayer has become so familiar to many Christians that they no longer think about the meaning of the words they're reciting, ironically and unknowingly disobeying Jesus' command not to pray with "empty phrases" (Matt. 6:7).

Understanding the overarching structure of the prayer can help us better understand the meaning of individual petitions. The petitions in the prayer are divided into two categories: (1) Godward petitions focusing on God's honor, and (2) manward petitions focusing on human needs.

The first petitions repeat the pronoun "your" three times: (1) "hallowed be your name," (2) "your kingdom come," and (3) "your will be done." The second petitions include eight personal pronouns: (1) "Give us this day our daily bread," (2) "forgive us our debts, as we also have forgiven our debtors," and (3) "lead us not into temptation, but deliver us from evil."

It's also helpful to understand how the petitions relate to each other. For example, the first petition, "hallowed be your name," is best understood as the greatest of the three Godward petitions. We ask the Father to hallow his name by causing his kingdom to come and his will to be done on earth as it is in heaven.

The three subsequent manward petitions for daily bread, forgiveness, and protection from temptation and evil should be seen not as disconnected from the Godward petitions, but as the means to their fulfillment. We ask the Father to give us our daily bread, to forgive our sins, and to protect us from temptation and evil not ultimately for us—but so that we will hallow the Father's name by causing his kingdom to come and his will to be done on earth as it is in heaven.

Therefore, our study of the meaning of the Lord's Prayer and its applications to life and ministry will draw from this overall structure and its flow of thought found in the prayer.

Godward petitions for God's honor:

Hallowed be your name.
　Your kingdom come,
　Your will be done, on earth as it is in heaven.

Manward petitions for our needs:

Give us this day our daily bread,
　Forgive us our debts, as we also have forgiven our debtors.
　Lead us not into temptation, but deliver us from evil.

THE GODWARD and manward petitions should be seen as a whole. Augustine teaches that in the Godward petitions we "ask for eternal goods" and that in the manward petitions we "ask for temporal goods, which are, however, necessary for obtaining the eternal goods."[8]

THE PURPOSE of the Prayer

Jesus introduces all these petitions by saying, "Pray then like this" (Matt. 6:9). The Greek word translated "like this" (οὕτως) means to pray "after this manner"—instructing us not merely to recite these words in prayer, although that's acceptable, but to use them as a model for all our prayers.

Augustine teaches that praying in a "correct and proper way" means that we "say nothing that is not contained in the Lord's Prayer." So we pray using not only "these very words," but also "the other words we may prefer to say" that will help us follow the model of the Lord's Prayer.[9]

Obviously, we are not limited to praying only the exact words of the Lord's Prayer. There are many prayers in Scripture (e.g., in the Psalms) that use very different words. The point is that the Lord's Prayer is a model for our prayers. The prayers we bring to God are applications of the petitions in the Lord's Prayer.

For example, the Lord's Prayer says, "Your will be done." That authorizes us to pray specifically for all the ways in which we would like God's will to be done: "Lord, please defeat those who promote abortion in our land." "Lord, help me to be faithful as I talk to my family about Jesus."

---

8. Augustine, *Enchiridion on Faith, Hope, and Love*, 30.
9. Augustine writes, "It was very appropriate that all these truths [in the Lord's Prayer] should be entrusted to us to remember in *these very words.* [But] Whatever be *the other words we may prefer to say* (words which the one praying chooses so that his disposition may become clearer to himself or which he simply adopts so that his disposition may be intensified), we say nothing that is not contained in the Lord's Prayer, provided of course we are praying in a correct and proper way." *A letter to Proba by Saint Augustine, Bishop* (Ep. 130, 11, 21–12, 22: CSEL 44, 63–64) *On the Lord's Prayer.*

Jesus teaches us to follow this model in all our prayers so that we will understand that our purpose in life is the same as his—to hallow the Father's name by causing his kingdom to come and his will to be done on earth as it is in heaven. Jesus knows that to do this, we will need to be constantly trusting our heavenly Father for our daily bread, forgiveness, and deliverance from all the evil he came to conquer for our sake and for the sake of the Father's name.

Jesus wants us not only to believe in these truths with our minds, but also to embrace them in prayer with our heart affections so that we will live out our whole lives in light of them. Only then can we know the hope of the gospel that is the hope of God's glory, the hope of God's kingdom, and the hope of God's will being done on earth as in heaven.

Only then can we know the hope of God's promised provisions of our daily bread, forgiveness, and deliverance from evil —especially as we dare to follow Jesus in the suffering that always accompanies those who pray and then live like this.

CONCLUSION

But sadly, most people don't use the Lord's Prayer this way, if they use it at all. Seeing how people in his day abused the Lord's Prayer, Martin Luther called it "the greatest martyr on earth":

What a great pity that the prayer of such a master is prattled and chattered so irreverently all over the world! How many pray the Lord's Prayer several thousand times in the course of a year, and if they were to keep on doing so for a thousand years, they would not have tasted nor prayed one iota, one dot, of it! In a word, the Lord's Prayer is the greatest martyr on earth (as are the name and word of God). Everybody tortures and abuses it; few take comfort and joy in its proper use.[10]

Luther's harsh words against the abuses of the Lord's Prayer are rooted in his heartfelt longing for God's people to know and taste the riches that God brings to all who pray it. He writes:

> To this day I suckle at the Lord's Prayer like a child, and as an old man eat and drink from it and never get my fill. It is the very best prayer, even better than the psalter, which is so very dear to me. It is surely evident that a real master composed and taught it.[11]

Step Six: Answer the Review Questions with Answer Key

Try to answer the Review Questions below on your own before you refer to the Answer Key in the back of the book.

1. What are the historical contexts in which Jesus teaches this prayer in the books of Matthew and Luke?[i]
2. How are the petitions of the Lord's Prayer organized and related?[ii]
3. How should we use the Lord's Prayer when we pray?[iii]
4. What is the ultimate purpose of the Lord's Prayer?[iv]

---

10. Martin Luther, *Luther's Works*, ed. Gustav K. Wiencke (Fortress Press, 1968), 43:200.
11. Luther, *Luther's Works*, 43:200.

Step Seven: Answer the Discussion Questions with Sample Answers

Reflect on these questions either individually or in a group. They are intended to renew your understanding, stir your heart's desires, and deepen your love for God and others. Try to answer each question on your own before consulting the sample answers in the Answer Key.

1. Mind for Truth: How have you seen the Lord's Prayer neglected or misused?[v]
2. Heart for God: What shaping and reforming effects should the Lord's Prayer have on your heart?[vi]
3. Life for Ministry: What could it look like for you to grow in your love for God and others by praying through the Lord's Prayer?[vii]

Step Eight: Take the Review Quiz with Answer Key

This quiz is designed to help you recall and apply key concepts you're learning, increasing your understanding of these concepts for practical application in life and ministry. Try to answer each question on your own before you refer to the Answer Key.

1. What is the message context of the Lord's Prayer in Matthew?
   a. location during prayer
   b. heart motivations of prayer
   c. historical development of prayer
   d. persistence in prayer

2. What is the message context of the Lord's Prayer in Luke?

a. location during prayer

b. heart motivations of prayer

c. historical development of prayer

d. persistence in prayer

3. After Luke's account of the Lord's Prayer, Jesus teaches his disciples that the greatest ultimate answer to their prayers is which of the following?

a. the gift of wisdom

b. the Holy Spirit given to those who ask

c. a heightened awareness of God's activity in the world

d. a *yes* to the desires of their hearts

4. What is the ultimate focus of the first three petitions of the Lord's Prayer?

a. God's honor

b. human needs

c. God's will

d. God's kingdom

5. How do the manward petitions relate to the Godward petitions?

a. They are the means to fulfill them.

b. They are less important.

c. They are essentially the same.

d. They are less necessary.

6. What is our life purpose revealed in the Lord's Prayer?

a. to depend on the Lord for all things we need

b. to defeat the powers of darkness and spiritual authority

    c. to hallow the Father's name by causing his kingdom to come and will to be done

    d. to seek for eternal goods and not temporal goods

Answer Key

Chapter 1 Quiz answers are found in the Answer Key.[viii]

Step Nine: Meditate and Pray

All theology should lead us to doxology. The ultimate goal of learning biblical and theological truths is not just to renew our minds, but also to renew our heart affections so that our lives are renewed to the honor of God. Pause now to meditate on and pray about what God is teaching you in his Word. After you pray, consider recording any new insights for application later. Use this prayer outline below if you find it helpful.

- Praise God for how he deepens your hope in him and his purposes through the Lord's Prayer.
- Confess your failures to pray more regularly and to pray with right motivations.
- Thank the Lord for teaching you to pray in a way that aligns your life purpose more fully with his.
- Ask the Holy Spirit to align your prayers and heart affections more closely with the Lord's Prayer.

Step Ten: Go Deeper as a Lifelong Learner

This step encourages your deeper exploration by using key resources drawn from the chapter article and academic notes to help you grow in your understanding and application of biblical truths, promoting your lifelong learning and continued growth in spiritual maturity.

BIBLE PASSAGES

Gain a deeper understanding and application of the key biblical passages from the chapter article through more in-depth reading, reflection, study, memorization, and meditation.

"And rising very early in the morning, while it was still dark, he departed and went out to a desolate place, and there he prayed." (Mark 1:35)

"Beware of practicing your righteousness before other people in order to be seen by them, for then you will have no reward from your Father who is in heaven. . . . And when you pray, you must not be like the hypocrites. For they love to stand and pray in the synagogues and at the street corners, that they may be seen by others. Truly, I say to you, they have received their reward. But when you pray, go into your room and shut the door and pray to your Father who is in secret. And your Father who sees in secret will reward you. And when you pray, do not heap up empty phrases as the Gentiles do, for they think that they will be heard for their many words. Do not be like them. . . . Pray then like this: 'Our Father in heaven, hallowed be your name. Your kingdom come, your will be done, on earth as it is in heaven. Give us this day our daily bread, and forgive us our debts, as we also have forgiven our debtors. And lead us not into temptation, but deliver us from evil.'" (Matt. 6:1–13)

"Now Jesus was praying in a certain place, and when he finished, one of his disciples said to him, 'Lord, teach us to pray, as John taught his disciples.' And he said to them, 'When you pray, say: "Father, hallowed be your name. Your kingdom come. Give us each day our daily bread, and forgive us our sins, for we ourselves forgive everyone who is indebted to us. And lead us not into temptation."' And he said to them, 'Which of you who has a friend will go to him at midnight and say to him, "Friend, lend me three loaves, for a friend of mine has arrived on a journey, and I have nothing to set before him"; and he will answer from within, "Do not bother me; the door is now shut, and my children are with me in bed. I cannot get up and give you anything"? I tell you, though he will not get up and give him anything because he is his friend, yet because of his impudence he will rise and give him whatever he needs. And I tell you, ask, and it will be given to you; seek, and you will find; knock, and it will be opened to you. For everyone who asks receives, and the one who seeks finds, and to the one who knocks it will be opened. What father among you, if his son asks for a fish, will instead of a fish give him a serpent; or if he asks for an egg, will give him a scorpion? If you then, who are evil, know how to give good gifts to your children, how much more will the heavenly Father give the Holy Spirit to those who ask him!'" (Luke 11:1–13)

~

CATECHISMS

Explore key biblical truths through historic Christian cate-chisms that offer clear guidance on their meaning and life application.

Westminster Shorter Catechism (QQ. 98–99)

- Q. 98: What is prayer?
- A: Prayer is an offering up of our desires unto God, for things agreeable to his will, in the name of Christ, with confession of our sins, and thankful acknowledgment of his mercies.

- Q. 99: What rule hath God given for our direction in prayer?
- A: The whole word of God is of use to direct us in prayer; but the special rule of direction is that form of prayer which Christ taught his disciples, commonly called the Lord's prayer.

Heidelberg Catechism (QQ. 116–119)

- Q. 116: Why do Christians need to pray?
- A: Because prayer is the most important part of the thankfulness God requires of us. And also because God gives his grace and the Holy Spirit only to those who pray continually and groan inwardly, asking God for these gifts and thanking God for them.

- Q. 117: What is the kind of prayer that pleases God and that he listens to?
- A: First, we must pray from the heart to no other than the one true God, revealed to us in his Word, asking for everything God has commanded us to ask for. Second, we must fully recognize our need and misery, so that we humble ourselves in God's majestic presence. Third, we must rest on this unshakable foundation: even though we do not deserve it, God will surely listen to our prayer because of Christ our Lord. That is what God promised us in his Word.

- Q. 118: What did God command us to pray for?
- A: Everything we need, spiritually and physically, as embraced in the prayer Christ our Lord himself taught us.

- Q. 119: What is this prayer?
- A: Our Father in heaven, hallowed be your name. Your kingdom come. Your will be done, on earth as it is in heaven. Give us this day our daily bread. And forgive us our debts, as we also have forgiven our debtors. And do not bring us to the time of trial, but rescue us from the evil one. For the kingdom and the power and the glory are yours forever. Amen.

Study Tip: See the Westminster Larger Catechism (QQ. 178–196) for more detailed explanations.

BOOKS

Expand your understanding of key biblical concepts through selected books that offer more in-depth exploration and practical application.

- Thomas Watson, *The Lord's Prayer*—A foundational Puritan exposition of the Lord's Prayer, deeply theological and practical. Watson breaks down each petition with clarity and pastoral insight, making it one of the most respected works on the subject.

- Martin Luther, *A Simple Way to Pray*—Luther's personal guide on how to pray, focusing on the Lord's Prayer, Ten Commandments, and the Apostles' Creed. This is a valuable resource for understanding prayer within the historic Christian and Lutheran tradition.

- J. I. Packer, *Praying the Lord's Prayer*—A contemporary classic by a leading evangelical theologian, Packer explains the meaning and importance of each part of the Lord's Prayer, making it accessible to modern readers.

2

OUR FATHER'S NAME

Step One: Read the Introduction

Jesus begins his teaching on prayer by emphasizing the communal nature of the Christian faith as he instructs his disciples to address God not merely on their own behalf by saying, "*my* Father," but on the behalf of others by saying, "*our* Father."

Jesus added a new personal name for God in the New Testament. It is the name *Father* that is similar to the Aramaic word *Abba* used in Jesus' time as an endearing expression of a child for a loving father. Through faith in Christ, we are adopted into the life of God's family, and we are to pray as children relate to and speak with a loving father.

To help us strike a needed balance between understanding God's closeness to us as our loving Father and understanding God's transcendence as our sovereign King, Jesus also instructs us to pray to God as "our Father in *heaven*." The word *heaven* refers to the manifestation of God's invisible and transcendent presence—that God is both our all-loving heavenly Father and our all-powerful, sovereign King who is ruling over all things from heaven on our behalf.

Jesus then teaches us to ask our Father in heaven to hallow his name—to honor and set apart his name, to cause his name to be celebrated and esteemed as holy in our lives and in all nations. In doing so, Jesus means for us to develop a great passion and zeal for the Father's name, honor, and glory so that we will find our ultimate joy in life by worshipping him alone.

In this chapter, we will learn to ask our Father in heaven to honor his name in all things.

Step Two: Review the Learning Goals

Learning Goals

In this chapter, you will be equipped to:

- Pray as part of a church community in the bond of faith and as a child relating to a loving father.
- Pray to our heavenly Father as our transcendent King with humble respect and bold endearment.
- Ask our Father in heaven to hallow, honor, and set apart his name.
- Find in honoring the Father's name our ultimate joy in life.

Step Three: Review the Key Ideas

Key Ideas

In this chapter, these are the key ideas:

- Praying "*our* Father" emphasizes the communal nature of the Christian faith and reveals the familial relationship we have with God.

- Praying "our Father *in heaven*" balances our views of God as Father and King.
- Hallowing God's name means honoring God for who he is and what he does and asking him to honor and vindicate his name.
- Hallowing God's name means finding our ultimate joy in life by worshipping him alone.

Step Four: Answer the Reflection Questions

Take a moment before reading the chapter article to reflect on these questions. They'll help you connect your beliefs, desires, and practices with the topics ahead, allowing for deeper engagement and more practical application to your life and ministry.

1. How does the way that you address God in prayer affect how you pray?
2. What do you think it means to honor God's name?

Step Five: Read the Chapter Article with Academic Notes

Jesus begins his teaching on prayer by instructing his disciples to address God not merely on their own behalf, but on the behalf of others by saying, "*Our* Father"—not "*My* Father." [1]

Likewise, Jesus teaches that we should not pray "Give *me* this day *my* daily bread" but "Give *us* this day *our* daily bread," and not "forgive *me my* debts as *I* also have forgiven *my* debtors" but "forgive *us our* debts, as *we* also have forgiven *our* debtors." And he does not teach us to pray "lead *me* not into

---

1. Jesus' emphasis on praying to the Father does not mean that we should not also pray to the Son and the Holy Spirit. In the Lord's Prayer, Jesus invites his followers to join with him in the intra-Trinitarian fellowship of the Godhead as the Father glorifies his name through the Son by the power of his Holy Spirit.

temptation, but deliver *me* from evil" but "lead *us* not into temptation, but deliver *us* from evil."

Jesus is not forbidding his followers to address God as "*my* Father." He also referred to God as "*My* Father" (John 5:17), and he said, "I am ascending to *my* Father and *your* Father, to *my* God and *your* God" (20:17).

Nor is Jesus forbidding private prayer or prayer for one's own needs. Just before giving his disciples these petitions, he encouraged them to pray privately: "when you pray, go into your room and shut the door and pray to your Father who is in secret" (Matt. 6:6).

By instructing his disciples to pray by using the pronouns *our*, *us*, and *we* instead of *me*, *my*, and *I* throughout the prayer, Jesus is emphasizing the communal nature of the Christian faith and the bond of unity in the family of God and the body of Christ as a group, as the nucleus of the future church. And he is telling them how the church ought to pray together.[2]

OUR FATHER

Jesus then teaches his disciples to address God in their communal prayers for each other as "our *Father*" to impress on them what the God they are praying to is like. Throughout Scripture, God reveals what he is like by revealing his names.

Before the time of Moses, God revealed what he was like by using simple, general Hebrew names, like El (אֵל), Elohim (אֱלֹהִים), El Shaddai (אֵל שַׁדַּי), translated as "God" and "God

---

2. Augustine saw the Lord's Prayer as beginning with an implicit declaration that we're all one spiritual family: "You then who have found a Father in heaven, be loth to cleave to the things of earth. For you are about to say, 'Our Father, which art in heaven.' You have begun to belong to a great family." Augustine, *Sermon 9 on the New Testament*, in *Nicene and Post-Nicene Fathers, First Series*, vol. 6, ed. by Philip Schaff (Christian Literature Publishing, 1888), accessed July 27, 2024, https://www.newadvent.org/fathers/160309.htm

Almighty." These names reveal God's sovereign power and might, and his transcendent nature as the Creator and Ruler who is high and lifted up in heaven over all things.

Later God reveals himself to Moses by using his Hebrew name יהוה (transliterated as YHWH—Yahweh) to show that he is also a personal, faithful, covenant-keeping God of grace who promises to deliver his people by his great power (Ex. 3:15).

By giving himself a personal name, God reveals that he is a person and not an impersonal force or higher power.[3] In the New Testament, God retains many of these Old Testament names and translates his personal name YHWH as LORD, using the Greek word κύριος (*kurios*) and applying that to Jesus.

But a new personal name for God is added by Jesus Christ. It is the name *Father*, from the Greek word *Pater* (Πάτερ), similar to the Aramaic word *Abba* used in Jesus' time as an endearing expression of a child for a loving father.[4]

Abba was not normally used for God by the Jews of Jesus' day, so they were angry when Jesus spoke of God as "my Father [Abba]" and taught his followers to do the same in a way that implied, in their view, that Christ-followers' relationship with God was closer than that of other Israelites (John 5:17–18).[5]

---

3. Bavinck writes, "YHWH is the highest revelation of God in the Old Testament. YHWH is God's real, personal name." Herman Bavinck, *Reformed Dogmatics*, vol. 2, *God and Creation*, ed. John Bolt, trans. John Vriend (Baker Academic, 2004), 95.

4. God is sometimes compared to a father in the Old Testament (Ps. 103:13). But most of the Old Testament references to God's fatherhood are references to the entire Trinity, not just the person of the Father (Deut. 32:6; Isa. 63:16; 64:8; Acts 7:24–29). In Isaiah 9:6, "Everlasting Father" is a title of the coming Messiah. According to Bavinck, "'Father' is thus the supreme revelation of God, and since the Father is made known to us by Jesus through the Spirit, the full, abundant revelation of God's name is now Trinitarian: Father, Son, and Holy Spirit." *Reformed Dogmatics*, 97.

5. In the Old Testament, God is referred to as Israel's Father (i.e., "our Father" in Isaiah 64:8, "your Father" in Deuteronomy 32:6) but Israelites were never told to address God personally as "my Father." Regarding Jesus' practice of addressing God as Father using the Aramaic term, *Abba*, German Lutheran

In the Sermon on the Mount, Jesus refers to God as *Father* seventeen times as he teaches his followers about the life and values of all who trust in God *as their Father in heaven*.[6] And as Jesus suffered in the garden of Gethsemane, he prayed to God, saying, "Abba, Father, all things are possible for you" (Mark 14:36).

The name *Father* indicates God's astonishing familial relationship with his people through Jesus Christ.[7] The New Testament teaches that followers of Jesus share in the relationship that Jesus *the* Son has with God *his* Father. This means that the

---

theologian and New Testament scholar Joachim Jeremias (1900–1979) writes: "It is quite unusual that Jesus should have addressed God as 'my Father'; it is even more so that he should have used the Aramaic form Abba.... It can certainly be said that there is no instance of the use of Abba as an address to God in all the extensive prayer-literature of Judaism, whether in liturgical or in private prayers.... All this confronts us with a fact of fundamental importance. We do not have a single example of God being addressed as Abba in Judaism, but Jesus always addressed God in this way in his prayers. The only exception is the cry from the cross (Mark 15:34; Matt. 27:46), and the reason for that is its character as a quotation.... If we keep in mind this setting for Abba it will be clear why Palestinian Judaism does not use Abba as a form of address to God. Abba was a children's word, used in everyday talk, an expression of courtesy. It would have seemed disrespectful, indeed unthinkable, to the sensibilities of Jesus' contemporaries to address God with the familiar word. Jesus dared to use Abba as a form of address to God. This Abba is the *ipsissima vox Jesu* [the very voice of Jesus].... The complete novelty and uniqueness of Abba as an address to God in the prayers of Jesus shows that it expresses the heart of Jesus' relationship to God. He spoke to God as a child to its father: confidently and securely, and yet at the same time reverently and obediently." Joachim Jeremias, *New Testament Theology: The Proclamation of Jesus*, trans. John Bowden (Charles Scribner's Sons, 1971), 64–67.

6. In the part of his sermon that addresses anxiety, Jesus gives beautiful illustrations of the Father's care for nature, including birds and flowers, which the Father values far less than his beloved children (Matt. 6:25–34).

7. In the New Testament, the name *Father* becomes the regular name for the first person of the Trinity, the person who sent Jesus into the world. The apostles followed Jesus' example and teaching by using the word *Father* in reference to the first person of the Trinity, who is distinct from the Son and the Holy Spirit (John 1:14, 18; 5:17–26; 14:16–17; Gal. 4:6; 2 Peter 1:17; 2 John 9).

love that God has for all who are in Christ by faith is the same love that the Father has for his one and only Son.

Through faith in Christ, we're adopted into the life of God's family. God the Father becomes our Father, and God the Son becomes our elder brother.[8] We who were once enemies of and strangers to God are now in the high position of being his own beloved children.[9] Paul writes, "You have received the Spirit of adoption as sons, by whom we cry, 'Abba! Father!'" (Rom. 8:15).

To be considered right with God the Judge is wonderful, but to be adopted, loved, and cared for by God the Father is even greater.[10] According to the apostle John, "To all who did receive him [Jesus], who believed in his name, he gave the right to become *children of God*" (John 1:12).

One of the treasured rights as adopted children of God is our immediate and full access into God's loving presence through prayer.[11] Jesus knew that the only way for his followers to enter into the fullness of their relationship with God through him, without being crippled by their fear of God's punishment

---

8. The resurrected Jesus said to his disciples, "I am ascending to *my Father* and *your Father*, to *my God* and *your God*" (John 20:17).

9. God declares that all who are in Christ have a relationship with him as his deeply loved and adopted children. The goal of Jesus' death for us is "to redeem those who were under the law, so that we might receive adoption as sons" (Gal. 4:5). Paul also teaches that the ultimate goal of God's election is adoption. "In love he predestined us for adoption to himself as sons through Jesus Christ" (Eph. 1:4–5).

10. J. I. Packer writes, "If you want to judge how well a person understands Christianity, find out how much he makes of the thought of being God's child, and having God as his Father. If this is not the thought that prompts and controls his worship and prayers and his whole outlook on life, it means that he does not understand Christianity very well at all." J. I. Packer, *Knowing God* (InterVarsity Press, 1993), 201.

11. Jesus knew that the result of his followers' believing that God is their loving heavenly Father would be that they would pray with the persistent, shameless boldness of dearly beloved children as he did. This is how the apostle John describes the effect of believing this: "perfect love casts out fear" (1 John 4:18).

for their sin, was by their first knowing how deeply God loves them as a father loves his own children.

Therefore, Jesus teaches his followers not to look to the eloquent prayers of the religious professionals as examples of how to pray, relate to, and speak with their loving Father. Only then will their prayers be genuine, heartfelt, and sincere, because they know that their Father will always care for them and give good things to his children who ask (Matt. 7:9–11).

OUR FATHER in Heaven

This biblical concept of our closeness and intimacy with God as "Abba, Father" does not imply a lack of reverence toward God. We must always have a healthy tension between bold endearment and humble respect when addressing God as "our Father."

To help us strike the needed balance between under-standing God's closeness to us as our loving Father and under-standing God's transcendence as our sovereign King, Jesus instructs us to pray to God as "our Father *in heaven*."

The word *heaven* in Scripture has several meanings. It can denote the sky with clouds, God's presence, or the state of angels and humans as they share God's presence. Jesus' reference to heaven in this prayer is to the manifestation of God's invisible and transcendent presence, sometimes referred to in Scripture as God's kingly dwelling place and his throne room.[12]

The Bible teaches that God's presence is everywhere in the universe—called "the heavens and the earth" that God created in the beginning (Psalm 139; Gen. 1:1). But the concept of *heaven*

---

12. Early in his ministry, Jesus said, "I have come *down from heaven*, not to do my own will but the will of him who sent me" (John 6:38). At the end of his earthly ministry, the disciples watched the resurrected Jesus return to heaven: "As they were looking on, he was lifted up, and a cloud took him out of their sight" (Acts 1:9).

that Jesus uses in this prayer is that of God's uniquely displaying his presence in the universe.

In the beginning, before the fall, God's presence was uniquely displayed on earth with Adam and Eve in the garden paradise. It was literally "heaven on earth." God is described as "walking in the garden in the cool of the day" (Gen. 3:8). There was no pain, suffering, disease, sickness, or death. The Hebrew prophets use the word *shalom* to describe this state of full peace, completeness, wholeness, and blessedness.

But because of the fall of humanity in sin, the fullness of God's holy presence and blessing on earth had to be withdrawn. Heaven and earth are now tragically separated. The accomplishment of God's will continues to be done perfectly in heaven, but no longer on the earth. This is why there is so much pain, suffering, disease, sickness, and death on the earth.

Apart from redemption, God is no longer down here on the earth "with us" as he was in the beginning. Instead, because of sin, God is pictured in the Bible as the transcendent, almighty God who is now "up above" in heaven sitting on his throne, declaring, "*Heaven* is my throne, and the *earth* is my footstool" (Isa. 66:1; Acts 7:49).[13]

In the meantime, Jesus instructs his followers to address God in their prayers as he does—with the intimacy of a child coming up into the lap of a merciful, loving father, and the respect and reverence of a servant bowing before the throne of his powerful, sovereign king.

By instructing us to address God in prayer as "our Father in heaven," Jesus teaches us to address God who is *both* our all-loving Father who is near us *and* our all-powerful, sovereign King who is ruling over all things from heaven on our behalf.[14]

---

13. The apostle Paul teaches that God's redemptive plan in Jesus Christ is to restore cosmic wholeness by unifying heaven and earth again in the Messiah (Eph. 1:9–10) so that once again God would be "all in all" (1 Cor. 15:28).
14. One of the ancient dilemmas regarding a proper understanding of God

. . .

HALLOWED BE Your Name

Jesus then teaches us to ask our Father in heaven for three things that are related to (1) his name, (2) his kingdom, and (3) his will.

The Greek phrase that is translated "hallowed be your name" (ἁγιασθήτω τὸ ὄνομά σου) is difficult to translate accurately.[15] Since this is a petition to God, the best way that it can be expressed in English is to pray something like this: "hallow your name!" As strange as it may seem at first, we are to ask the Father to hallow his own name.

What does *hallow* mean? The Greek word (ἁγιασθήτω) translated by the Old English term "hallow" means "to set something apart," "to sanctify it," and thereby "to make it holy." So to ask our Father to hallow his name means that we ask him to "set apart his name," "sanctify his name," and thereby "cause his name to be celebrated and esteemed as holy."

The concept of *God's name* is used throughout the Bible to describe the revelation of God's Being and presence.[16] In Scripture, God's name is inseparable from his person; it reflects his very essence—who he is and what he does. This is why God's name is described in the Bible as especially sacred.

---

involves understanding the relationship of God's merciful love as a Father to his sovereign power as a heavenly King—especially when his people are suffering.

15. This is because ἁγιασθήτω τὸ ὄνομά σου is in the third-person singular aorist passive imperative and there is no exact English equivalent to express a passive imperative in the third person. We are used to seeing imperatives in the first and second person as commands, e.g., "Go dig a hole!" But a Greek third-person imperative expresses strongly that an action should be taken: "May a hole be dug!" And since this first petition uses the imperative of request ἁγιασθήτω as a prayer to God, it is asking and strongly calling on God to hallow his own name.

16. The name of God signifies: (1) God himself (Pss. 5:11; 9:2, 10; 116:13; 1 Kings 5:5), (2) the will and authority of God (1 Sam. 17:45; Matt. 28:19), and (3) the object of our trust in and profession of God (Acts 2:38; 21:13).

To hallow God's name means to set God apart and honor him for who he is in the fullness of his attributes and for what he does in the creation, redemption, and restoration of all things in Jesus Christ by his Holy Spirit. God's name is hallowed when he is exalted and when he receives the honor and glory that he alone deserves as the Creator, Redeemer, and Restorer of all things in Christ.

The opposite of hallowing God's name is profaning his name by *not* honoring and worshipping God for who he is and what he does. God declared to Moses, *"I will be sanctified*, and before all the people *I will be glorified"* (Lev. 10:3). But when Israel rebelled against God by disobeying his commands, he told Moses, "Speak to Aaron and his sons . . . so that they do not *profane my holy name*. . . . You shall not *profane my holy name*, that I may be sanctified among the people of Israel" (22:2, 32).[17]

Israel's disobedience, apostasy, and exile caused God's name to be profaned and mocked by all the other nations of the world, since Israel had been named as God's people. In response to Israel's profaning of God's name, God promises, through the prophet Ezekiel, to honor and vindicate his own name among the nations:

> And I will vindicate the holiness of my great name, which has been profaned among the nations, and which you have profaned among them. And the nations will know that I am the LORD, declares the Lord GOD, when through you I vindicate my holiness before their eyes. (Ezek. 36:23)

---

17. See also the reason for God's declaration of judgment against Sidon and Gog: "Thus says the Lord GOD: 'Behold, I am against you, O Sidon, and *I will manifest my glory in your midst*. And they shall know that I am the LORD when I execute judgments in her and *manifest my holiness* in her. So I will *show my greatness and my holiness* and make myself known in the eyes of many nations. Then they will know that I am the LORD" (Ezek. 28:22; 38:23). Here it is God's name, LORD, that is at issue.

Likewise, in this first petition of the Lord's Prayer, Jesus teaches us to keep asking our Father in heaven to honor and vindicate his own name that is being profaned among the nations by their disobedience to his will. Throughout Scripture, we learn that God has a great passion and zeal for his own name, honor, and glory. In Isaiah 48:9–11, God proclaims to his people Israel:

> For my name's sake I defer my anger; for the sake of my praise I restrain it for you, that I may not cut you off. . . . For my own sake, for my own sake, I do it, for how should my name be profaned? My glory I will not give to another.

The most passionate heart to see God's name honored among all nations is God's heart. When God sees his name being profaned by the nations through their worship of false gods, it awakens his holy and jealous zeal for them and for their worship. God's holy jealousy for their worship is rooted in his knowledge that he created them so that they can find ultimate happiness and joy in life only by worshipping him alone.

Throughout the Bible, we learn that God's ultimate purpose for all things is to display the honor and glory of his name.

- God created us *for his glory* (Isa. 43:6–7).
- God chose his people *for his glory* (Eph. 1:4–6, 12, 14).
- God rescued Israel from Egypt *for his glory* (Ps. 106:7–8).
- God restored Israel from exile *for the glory of his name* (Ezek. 36:22–23, 32).
- Jesus teaches us to do good works *for the Father's glory* (Matt. 5:16).
- Jesus teaches that God answers prayer *so that the Father will be glorified* (John 14:13).

- God struck Herod dead because he did not *give God glory* (Acts 12:23).
- God forgives our sins *for his own sake* (Ps. 25:11; Isa. 43:25).
- God instructs us to do everything *for his glory* (1 Cor. 6:20; 10:31).
- Jesus is coming again *for the glory of God* (2 Thess. 1:9–10).
- God's plan is to fill the earth with the knowledge *of his glory* (Hab. 2:14).
- In the new heaven and earth, the sun will be replaced by *God's glory* (Rev. 21:23).

CONCLUSION

God's primary purpose for creating the world is so that all the nations would glorify, worship, and find their joy in him. This is why we exist—to glorify God by enjoying him and helping to extend the worship and enjoyment of God to all nations.

The Christian hope is that when Jesus returns, he will make all things new so that God the Father will be honored and glorified in everything forever (1 Cor. 15:24–25, 28). In the meantime, Jesus calls us to join with him and pray to our Father in heaven that his name would be hallowed.

Step Six: Answer the Review Questions with Answer Key

Try to answer the Review Questions below on your own before you refer to the Answer Key in the back of the book.

1. How should the phrase "our Father" change your view of being a follower of Jesus Christ?[i]

2. How should the phrase "in heaven" affect your understanding and use of the Lord's Prayer?[ii]
3. How does the phrase "hallowed be your name" help shape your attitude toward God in prayer?[iii]
4. What is God's primary purpose for creating the world and humanity?[iv]

Step Seven: Answer the Discussion Questions with Sample Answers

Reflect on these questions either individually or in a group. They are intended to renew your understanding, stir your heart's desires, and deepen your love for God and others. Try to answer each question on your own before consulting the sample answers in the Answer Key.

1. Mind for Truth: How should addressing God as *Father* in the Lord's Prayer deepen your understanding of him?[v]
2. Heart for God: In what specific ways has your relationship with God changed your prayers, such as the topics you address or the attitudes you bring?[vi]
3. Life for Ministry: How does God's own zeal and passion to see his name honored affect the way you live?[vii]

Step Eight: Take the Review Quiz with Answer Key

This quiz is designed to help you recall and apply key concepts you're learning, increasing your understanding of these concepts for practical application in life and ministry. Try to answer each question on your own before you refer to the Answer Key.

· · ·

1. Why does Jesus instruct his disciples to pray using plural pronouns like *our*, *us*, and *we*?

    a. to protect them from addressing God as "my Father"

    b. to discourage them from praying for their personal needs

    c. to emphasize the communal nature of the Christian faith

    d. to remind them of the presence of the Holy Spirit during their prayers

2. Why were the Jews of Jesus' day upset when Jesus called God "Father" and taught his followers to do the same?

    a. It implied that followers of Christ were closer to God than they were.

    b. It lessened the glory of God by appealing to human fatherhood.

    c. There was no theological basis in the Torah for God's being considered a "Father."

    d. Seeing God as Father seemed disharmonious with the idea of God as Divine Judge.

3. Which word found in the Lord's Prayer balances the nearness of God the Father by illustrating his transcendence?

    a. *hallowed*

    b. *name*

    c. *your*

    d. *heaven*

4. What does the word *heaven* in the Lord's Prayer mean?

    a. the sky with clouds

    b. outer space

    c. God's immanent presence

    d. the state of those sharing in God's presence

e. God's invisible and transcendent presence

5. What does the word *hallow* mean?
   a. set apart
   b. cause to be beyond comprehension
   c. proclaim
   d. defend

6. What is God's ultimate purpose for all things?
   a. that they would be fruitful and multiply
   b. that they would display the honor and glory of his name
   c. that they would live in fullness now
   d. that they would pass away to reveal his permanent glory

Answer Key

Chapter 2 quiz answers are found in the Answer Key.[viii]

Step Nine: Meditate and Pray

All theology should lead us to doxology. The ultimate goal of learning biblical and theological truths is not just to renew our minds, but also to renew our heart affections so that our lives are renewed to the honor of God. Pause now to meditate on and pray about what God is teaching you in his Word. After you pray, consider recording any new insights for application later. Use this prayer outline below if you find it helpful.

- Praise God for revealing himself as "our Father" and enabling you to worship him in spirit and truth.
- Confess the ways that you profane the Father's name and seek things other than his glory.

- Thank Jesus for redeeming you and bringing you into the family of God so that you can pray to our Father in heaven.
- Ask the Holy Spirit to restore your heart and this world so that the Father's name is hallowed more completely.

Here is an example of how you can pray through the petition "Our Father in heaven, hallowed be your name" in the Lord's Prayer. You can use this as a guide during personal devotions, with your family, in small groups, or with your congregation.

> *Our Father in heaven, we come before you as our loving Father who cares for us with an everlasting love, and as our sovereign King who reigns over all things from your heavenly throne to carry out your good and perfect will in our lives and in the whole world. We ask you to hallow your name on earth as it is now hallowed in heaven where angels ceaselessly bring praise, honor, and glory to you for the greatness of who you are and for all that you do in your magnificent acts of creation and redemption. Honor your name in and through our lives by deepening our knowledge of you, strengthening our love for you, and increasing our joy and delight in you above all else.*

Step Ten: Go Deeper as a Lifelong Learner

This step encourages your deeper exploration by using key resources drawn from the chapter article and academic notes to help you grow in your understanding and application of biblical truths, promoting your lifelong learning and continued growth in spiritual maturity.

Gain a deeper understanding and application of the key biblical passages from the chapter article through more in-depth reading, reflection, study, memorization, and meditation.

God created us for his glory.

> "I will say to the north, Give up, and to the south, Do not with-hold; bring my sons from afar and my daughters from the end of the earth, everyone who is called by my name, whom I created for my glory, whom I formed and made." (Isa. 43:6–7)

God chose us for his glory.

> "He chose us in him before the foundation of the world, that we should be holy and blameless before him. In love he predestined us for adoption to himself as sons through Jesus Christ, according to the purpose of his will, to the praise of his glorious grace, with which he has blessed us in the Beloved. . . . We who were the first to hope in Christ might be to the praise of his glory. . . . The promised Holy Spirit . . . is the guarantee of our inheritance until we acquire possession of it, to the praise of his glory." (Eph. 1:4–6, 12–14)

God rescued Israel from Egypt for his glory.

> "Our fathers, when they were in Egypt, did not consider your wondrous works; they did not remember the abundance of your steadfast love, but rebelled by the sea, at the Red Sea. Yet

he saved them for his name's sake, that he might make known his mighty power." (Ps. 106:7–8)

God restored Israel from exile for the glory of his name.

"Therefore say to the house of Israel, Thus says the Lord GOD: It is not for your sake, O house of Israel, that I am about to act, but for the sake of my holy name, which you have profaned among the nations to which you came. And I will vindicate the holiness of my great name, which has been profaned among the nations, and which you have profaned among them. And the nations will know that I am the LORD, declares the Lord GOD, when through you I vindicate my holiness before their eyes. . . . It is not for your sake that I will act, declares the Lord GOD; let that be known to you. Be ashamed and confounded for your ways, O house of Israel." (Ezek. 36:22–23, 32)

Jesus teaches us to do good works for the Father's glory.

"In the same way, let your light shine before others, so that they may see your good works and give glory to your Father who is in heaven." (Matt. 5:16)

God answers prayer so that the Father will be glorified.

"Whatever you ask in my name, this I will do, that the Father may be glorified in the Son." (John 14:13)

God struck Herod dead because he did not give God glory.

"Immediately an angel of the Lord struck him down, because he did not give God the glory, and he was eaten by worms and breathed his last." (Acts 12:23)

God forgives our sins for his own sake.

> "For your name's sake, O LORD, pardon my guilt, for it is great." (Ps. 25:11)

> "I, I am he who blots out your transgressions for my own sake, and I will not remember your sins." (Isa. 43:25)

God instructs us to do everything for his glory.

> "You were bought with a price. So glorify God in your body." (1 Cor. 6:20)

> "So, whether you eat or drink, or whatever you do, do all to the glory of God." (1 Cor. 10:31)

Jesus is coming again for the glory of God.

> "They will suffer the punishment of eternal destruction, away from the presence of the Lord and from the glory of his might, when he comes on that day to be glorified in his saints, and to be marveled at among all who have believed, because our testimony to you was believed." (2 Thess. 1:9–10)

> "Then comes the end, when he delivers the kingdom to God the Father after destroying every rule and every authority and power. For he must reign until he has put all his enemies under his feet. . . . When all things are subjected to him, then the Son himself will also be subjected to him who put all things in subjection under him, that God may be all in all. "(1 Cor. 15:24–25, 28)

God's plan is to fill the earth with the knowledge of his glory.

"For the earth will be filled with the knowledge of the glory of the Lᴏʀᴅ as the waters cover the sea." (Hab. 2:14)

God's glory will replace the sun in the new heaven and earth.

"And the city has no need of sun or moon to shine on it, for the glory of God gives it light, and its lamp is the Lamb." (Rev. 21:23)

CATECHISMS

Explore key biblical truths through historic Christian catechisms that offer clear guidance on their meaning and life application.

Westminster Shorter Catechism (Q. 101)

- Q. 101: What do we pray for in the first petition?
- A: In the first petition, which is, *Hallowed be thy name*, we pray that God would enable us and others to glorify him in all that whereby he maketh himself known, and that he would dispose all things to his own glory.

Westminster Larger Catechism (Q. 190)

- Q. 190: What do we pray for in the first petition?
- A: In the first petition (which is, Hallowed be thy name), acknowledging the utter inability and indisposition that is in ourselves and all men to honor God aright, we pray, that God would by his grace enable and incline us and others to know, to

acknowledge, and highly to esteem him, his titles, attributes, ordinances, word, works, and whatsoever he is pleased to make himself known by; and to glorify him in thought, word, and deed: that he would prevent and remove atheism, ignorance, idolatry, profaneness, and whatsoever is dishonorable to him; and, by his overruling providence, direct and dispose of all things to his own glory.

Heidelberg Catechism (Q. 122)

- Q. 122: What does the first petition mean?
- A: "Hallowed be your name" means: Help us to truly know you, to honor, glorify, and praise you for all your works and for all that shines forth from them: your almighty power, wisdom, kindness, justice, mercy, and truth. And it means, Help us to direct all our living—what we think, say, and do—so that your name will never be blasphemed because of us but always honored and praised.

New City Catechism (Q. 41)

- Q. 41: What does the first petition mean?
- A: Hallowed be your name means help us to honor, worship, and praise you in all that we do and live our lives so that others would see the goodness of your name and glory.

BOOKS

Expand your understanding of key biblical concepts

through selected books that offer more in-depth exploration and practical application.

- Jonathan Edwards, *The End for Which God Created the World*—Edwards's treatise delves into the ultimate purpose of creation: the glorification of God. His reflections on God's name being hallowed are foundational for understanding the broader cosmic significance of this petition in the Lord's Prayer.

- J. I. Packer, *Knowing God*—Packer's writing on the fatherhood of God, especially his chapter called "Sons of God," reflects on the intimacy and reverence encapsulated in the term "our Father." He explains the balance of awe and closeness in Christian prayer and how God's fatherhood should help shape all aspects of our lives.

- John Piper, *Desiring God: Meditations of a Christian Hedonist*—Piper reflects Jonathan Edwards's teaching that God is most glorified in us when we are most satisfied in him. He connects the idea of glorifying God with finding our ultimate joy in God's supreme worth and holiness.

HYMNS

Allow these biblical truths to lead you to praise and worship God with prayers and hymns that honor God for who he is and what he does.

- "Holy, Holy, Holy! Lord God Almighty," by Reginald Heber—This hymn celebrates the eternal holiness of the triune God, reflecting the heavenly worship described in Revelation 4. It invites worshipers to hallow God's name by glorifying God's triune holiness and majesty.

- "Be Thou My Vision" (ancient Irish hymn), author unknown—A heartfelt hymn that portrays God as a loving Father, central to the believer's life, providing wisdom, protection, and strength. The hymn balances intimacy and reverence, recognizing God as both a caring Father and a sovereign King, worthy of all praise.

- "Immortal, Invisible, God Only Wise," by Walter Chalmers Smith—This hymn highlights God's transcendence, wisdom, majesty, and holiness as our "Father of glory, pure Father of light," calling us to honor his name by acknowledging his supreme greatness over all things.

OUR FATHER'S KINGDOM AND WILL

Step One: Read the Introduction

The good news of God's kingdom is that the Father's creation, ruined by the fall, is being redeemed by Christ and restored by the Holy Spirit into the kingdom of God on earth. As our Redeemer King, Jesus lived the life we should have lived and died the death that we deserve. God then raised him from the dead, proclaiming his ultimate victory over evil and inaugurating his new kingly rule on earth as Lord.

Jesus' work, his mission, was to glorify the Father by causing his kingdom to come and his will to be done on earth as it is in heaven. When we ask that our Father's will be done, we are asking our Father in heaven to align all our life purposes and desires with his *preceptive will* revealed in the Bible.

The final phrase, "on earth as it is in heaven" (Matt. 6:10), should be seen as a culmination of the first three petitions. Therefore, we are to pray that our Father's name would be hallowed on earth as it is in heaven *by* causing his kingdom to come and his will to be done on earth as it is in heaven.

In this chapter, we will learn to pray for God's kingdom and will to come on earth as it is in heaven.

Step Two: Review the Learning Goals

Learning Goals

In this chapter, you will be equipped to:

- Pray for our Father to honor his name by causing his kingdom to come.
- Pray for our Father's revealed will to be done on earth.
- Pray for God's name to be honored by the coming of his kingdom and will.

Step Three: Review the Key Ideas

Key Ideas

In this chapter, these are the key ideas:

- Praying for God's kingdom to come involves yearning for the restoration of his kingdom.
- We pray for God's preceptive (revealed) will, not his decretive will.
- We pray for God's revealed will on earth to be obeyed and ask God to align all our life purposes and will with his will revealed in the Bible.

Step Four: Answer the Reflection Questions

Take a moment before reading the chapter article to reflect on these questions. They'll help you connect your beliefs, desires, and practices with the topics ahead, allowing for deeper engagement and more practical application to your life and ministry.

1. What do you think it means to pray for God's kingdom to come?
2. What do you think it means to pray for God's will to be done?

Step Five: Read the Chapter Article with Academic Notes

The first three petitions of the Lord's Prayer are interconnected. We can't fully understand the meaning of the first petition, "hallowed be your name," apart from understanding the meaning of the second and third, "Your kingdom come" and "your will be done" (Matt. 6:9–10). This is because the Father's name is hallowed *by* the coming of his kingdom, and the way the Father's kingdom comes is *by* his will being done on the earth.

The structure and word order of these three petitions in the original Greek text of the New Testament can also help us understand their meaning. The original text reads like this:

- *sanctify*—your name (ἁγιασθήτω—τὸ ὄνομά σου)
- *cause to come*—your kingdom (ἐλθέτω—ἡ βασιλεία σου)
- *bring about*—your will (γενηθήτω—τὸ θέλημά σου)[1]

Jesus teaches his followers to ask their Father in heaven to sanctify his name by *causing his kingdom to come* and by *bringing about his will* on earth as it is in heaven.

. . .

---

1. The word γενηθήτω is the imperative form of γίνομαι, translated: "Let it come into being! Let it happen! Let it come about!"

YOUR KINGDOM COME

To understand the full meaning of the second petition, ("Cause your kingdom to come!"), we need to understand who God is and what God does to cause his kingdom to come on earth through his creation, redemption, and restoration of all things lost in the fall. This includes understanding the *good news of God's kingdom*—that the Father's creation, ruined by the fall, is being redeemed by Christ and restored by the Holy Spirit *into the kingdom of God on earth*.

The mostly Jewish audience to whom Jesus was teaching this prayer was waiting for God's promised King to come and deliver them from their oppression and suffering by defeating all their enemies and establishing his kingdom on the earth forever.

From the Old Testament Scriptures, they knew that God had created the world to be an eternal, utopian, cosmic display of his glory as he rules over everything *as Lord*. They also knew that God had created humanity to reflect his glory as they find their joy in him and in his mission to fill the earth and rule over it *as Lord*, so that the paradise of his perfect rule would extend on earth for eternity.

The Scriptures also taught, however, that evil had entered the story through Satan, who enticed humanity to sin. Paradise was lost. As a result, God allowed Satan to set up his kingdom in this fallen world and to rule over it. The apostle John writes, "The whole world *lies in the power of* the evil one" (1 John 5:19). Satan now declares himself to be lord over all of God's creation to rule over it for his evil purposes.

Therefore, in the first century, when Jesus began his ministry by proclaiming the good news that God's kingdom is "at hand" (Matt. 4:17), his Jewish listeners understood this to mean that God's kingdom *in heaven* was finally returning *to earth* in a new way through him.[2] Jesus' miraculous signs and wonders were seen as magnificent displays of how God's promised kingdom had already come to earth.

In Jesus' day, the Jews were oppressed by the Roman government. They longed for their promised Messiah King to come, set up his kingdom, and save them from their oppression. So they were excited when Jesus began his public ministry, calling them to "repent and believe in the gospel" and that "the time is fulfilled, and the kingdom of God is at hand" (Mark 1:15).

But the Jews soon learned that the kingdom that Jesus was inaugurating was not what they expected. The nature of his kingdom extended far beyond the boundaries of earthly Israel, for Jesus came to deliver people of all nations from their sinful rebellion against God.[3]

The Scriptures teach that Jesus' life, death, resurrection, and ascension demonstrate his victory as Lord over all the powers of evil, including his and our archenemies of the world, the sinful human nature, the devil, and death.

As our Redeemer King, Jesus lived the life we should have lived and died the death we deserve to die for our sin. Through Jesus' death, as Paul writes, "he disarmed the rulers and authorities and put them to open shame, by triumphing over them" (Col. 2:15). Then God raised him from the dead,

---

2. The Bible presents Jesus, the gospel, and the new community of Christ-followers as being deeply rooted in this historical Jewish context. This is why the message of the gospel is that Jesus came first as the promised Jewish Messiah, fulfilling God's covenant promises to the Jews. When the apostle Paul begins to explain the gospel to the mostly Gentile and Greek church in Rome, he writes, "For I am not ashamed of the gospel, for it is the power of God for salvation to everyone who believes, *to the Jew first* and also to the Greek" (Rom. 1:16).

3. To their amazement, the citizens of this new kingdom were no longer limited to the Jews but included Gentiles from all nations.

proclaiming his ultimate victory over evil and inaugurating his new kingly rule on earth as Lord.

But Paul's explanation of the gospel extends beyond Jesus' death and resurrection in the past (1 Cor. 15:3–4) to include Jesus' present and future rule as the ascended King over all things by the Spirit (vv. 25–28).

When Jesus returns as King, he will fill the earth with God's glory by bringing everything on earth in subjection to the Father's will, including death and Satan. Then as the obedient, incarnate Son, Jesus will deliver up to the Father the kingdom he established, including himself as its King, so "that God may be all in all"—so that God the Father would be honored and glorified in everything (1 Cor. 15:28).

In the meantime, Jesus instructs his followers to long for and pray for the time when God will fulfill his promise to return the fullness of his kingdom on earth forever—by asking our Father in heaven to honor his name by causing his kingdom to come.[4]

YOUR WILL BE DONE

In the third petition, Jesus instructs his followers to ask our Father in heaven to cause his will to be done on earth as it is in

---

4. Note the role of the church in the Heidelberg Catechism. Lord's Day 48, Question 123 states: "What is the second petition? Answer: Thy kingdom come; that is, so govern us by Thy word and Spirit, that we submit ourselves to You always more and more; *preserve and increase Thy Church*; destroy the works of the devil, every power that exalts itself against You, and all wicked devices formed against Thy Holy Word, until the fullness of Thy kingdom come, wherein Thou shalt be all in all" (emphasis added).

John Piper writes, "Prayer is primarily a wartime walkie-talkie for the mission of the church as it advances against the powers of darkness and unbelief. It is not surprising that prayer malfunctions when we try to make it a domestic intercom to call upstairs for more comforts in the den." John Piper, *Let the Nations Be Glad!: The Supremacy of God in Missions*, 3rd ed., ed. David Mathis (Baker Academic, 2010), 65.

heaven. Again, this petition can be fully understood only by seeing its relationship to the two preceding. Therefore, Jesus is instructing his followers to ask their Father in heaven to honor his name and cause his kingdom to come *by* causing his will to be done on earth as it is in heaven.[5]

The Bible presents the unfolding mission of the triune God as Creator, Redeemer, and Restorer of all things lost in humanity and creation because of the fall as *accomplishing the Father's will*. Although God the Son and God the Spirit are equal in power and authority with God the Father, the Bible presents the Son as carrying out the Father's will and the Spirit as empowering it.

The Bible tells the story of the triune God's accomplishment of the Father's will like this:

- God the Father *establishes* his good and perfect will by *creating* all things.
- God the Son *accomplishes* the Father's will by *redeeming* all things lost in the fall.
- God the Spirit *applies* the Father's will by *restoring* all things lost in the fall.

In Ephesians 1, the apostle Paul refers to the Father's will before creation (vv. 1–5), the Son's accomplishment of his will in redemption (vv. 6–10), and the Spirit's application of his will in sealing believers (vv. 11–14).

At the beginning of his ministry, Jesus said, "I have come down from heaven, not to do my own will but the will of him who sent me" (John 6:38). At the end of his life and ministry, Jesus prayed to the Father, "I glorified you on earth, having accomplished the work that you gave me to do" (17:4).

Jesus' work, his mission, was to glorify the Father by

---

5. This third petition is not included in Luke's record in Luke 11:2.

causing his kingdom to come and his will to be done on earth as it is in heaven. One of the reasons Jesus instructed his disciples to pray for the successful fulfillment of his mission was so that they would be swept up with him in his mission to accomplish the Father's will on earth as it is in heaven.

The phrase "as it is in heaven" refers to the angelic beings in heaven who always obey God's will perfectly, described in Psalm 103:21 as "all his hosts, his ministers, *who do his will.*" The perfect obedience of the angelic hosts to the Father's will in heaven is the standard that Jesus reveals for God's new humanity of his followers on earth.

The original image of God in Adam and Eve displayed itself in their perfect obedience to God's will. In the beginning they were, according to Augustine, "able not to sin."[6] So they flourished by finding true happiness in their relationship with God and with each other, as they obeyed God perfectly, carrying out his will on the earth.

Though Adam and Eve were created sinless, they were not in a state of unchangeable perfection. They were perfect but not complete because they had not yet fully developed as image bearers. They still needed to have their obedience to God's will tested (Gen. 2:16–17). Although they were "able not to sin," they had not yet reached the state of being "not able to sin."[7] Herman Bavinck describes it this way: "Adam, accordingly, stood at the beginning of his 'career' not at the end. His condition was provisional and temporary and could

---

6. Augustine, *On Correction and Grace*, in *A Select Library of the Nicene and Post-Nicene Fathers of the Christian Church, First Series*, ed. Philip Schaff, trans. Peter Holmes, vol. 5, (Christian Literature Publishing, 1887), 644. In the original Latin, "*posse non peccare.*"

7. Although they were able not to sin (*posse non peccare*), they had not yet reached the state of being not able to sin (*non posse peccare*).

not remain as it was. It . . . had to pass on [either] to higher glory or to sin and death."[8]

It's hard to imagine what the further history of the human race and creation would have been like if Adam and Eve had obeyed God's will and passed over into a higher state of glory where they were no longer "able to sin." It would have been an eternal utopia, an earth filled with humanity flourishing in their relationship with God and each other, as they carried out God's will perfectly on the earth for eternity.[9]

Followers of Jesus, however, will know what that will be like when he returns to bring the fullness of heaven back down to earth and restore fallen humanity and creation to God's original design. In our new resurrected bodies, our souls will experience what Adam and Eve never experienced in the garden— the glorious state of not even being able to sin. When we're in the new earth, we will perfectly obey God's will just like the angels in heaven.

But what is the Father's will?

God's will is described in two ways in Scripture. Theologians refer to these as "the two wills of God"—his *decretive will* and his *preceptive will*. God's decretive will describes his sovereign and mysterious purposes at work in the world through which he ordains everything that comes to pass. God's preceptive will describes God's revealed moral instruction in the Bible that helps us know God's heart and desires.

When we ask our Father in heaven to cause his will to be done on earth as it is in heaven, we're not asking him to change his *decretive will* by somehow causing his sovereign purposes to be in alignment with our desired purposes. Martin Luther writes, "The good and gracious will of God [God's decretive

---

8. Herman Bavinck, *Reformed Dogmatics*, vol. 2, *God and Creation*, ed. John Bolt, trans. John Vriend (Baker Academic, 2004), 564.

9. Anthony A. Hoekema, *Created in God's Image* (Eerdmans, 1994).

will] is done indeed without our prayer; but we pray in this petition that it may be done also among us."[10]

Instead, we're asking our Father in heaven to align all our life purposes and desires with his *preceptive will* revealed in the Bible. Jesus reveals the Father's will as God's moral law found in the Bible, especially the Ten Commandments. John Calvin describes the Ten Commandments as "the true and eternal rule of righteousness for all humanity and nations who wish to conform their lives to God's will."[11]

Jesus teaches his followers to "seek first the kingdom of God *and his righteousness*" (Matt. 6:33). We seek first God's kingdom when we seek first God's righteousness revealed in God's Word. That *righteousness* is what God wills to be realized on the earth as it is in heaven.

CONCLUSION: On Earth as It Is in Heaven

The final phrase "on earth as it is in heaven" (Matt. 6:10) should not be understood as limited to the third petition but should be seen as the culmination of all three. This is why we are to pray that our Father's name would be hallowed on earth as it is in heaven by causing his kingdom to come and his will to be done on earth as it is in heaven.

Jesus teaches his followers to pray these petitions for the

---

10. "Question: What is meant by 'Your will be done'? Answer: The good and gracious will of God is done indeed without our prayer; but we pray in this petition that it may be done also among us. Question: How is this done? Answer: When God breaks and hinders every evil counsel and purpose, which would not let us hallow God's name nor let His kingdom come, such as the will of the devil, the world, and our own flesh; but strengthens and keeps us steadfast in His Word and in faith unto our end. This is His gracious and good will." Martin Luther, *The Book of Concord: The Confessions of the Evangelical Lutheran Church*, ed. Robert Kolb and Timothy J. Wengert, trans. Charles Arand et al. (Fortress Press, 2000), The First Petition, 495.

11. John Calvin, *Institutes of the Christian Religion*, trans. Henry Beveridge (Hendrickson Publishers, 2008), 4.20.15.

Father's name, kingdom, and will first, before they pray for their daily bread, forgiveness, and deliverance from evil. Luther shares the reason why: "If we are to be preserved and delivered from all evil, the name of God must be sanctified in us, his kingdom must be with us and his will be done among us."[12]

Step Six: Answer the Review Questions with Answer Key

Try to answer the Review Questions below on your own before you refer to the Answer Key in the back of the book.

1. What were the Jews expecting when they heard that "the kingdom of God is at hand"?[i]
2. What role does the Holy Spirit play in the fulfillment of God's will?[ii]
3. How will the state of resurrected believers in the world to come differ from the pre-fall state of Adam and Eve?[iii]
4. What is the difference between God's decretive will and his preceptive will?[iv]

Step Seven: Answer the Discussion Questions with Sample Answers

Reflect on these questions either individually or in a group. They are intended to renew your understanding, stir your heart's desires, and deepen your love for God and others. Try to answer each question on your own before consulting the sample answers in the Answer Key.

1. Mind for Truth: How is praying for God's kingdom

---

12. Luther, *Book of Concord*, The Seventh and Last Petition, 508.

to come different than praying for his will to be done in your life?[v]

2. Heart for God: Which specific desires or feelings in your heart need to be more aligned with God's will for your life?[vi]

3. Life for Ministry: How can you specifically pray for your community (on earth) to reflect more of God's will in heaven?[vii]

Step Eight: Take the Review Quiz with Answer Key

This quiz is designed to help you recall and apply key concepts you're learning, increasing your understanding of these concepts for practical application in life and ministry. Try to answer each question on your own before you refer to the Answer Key.

1. WHAT DID JESUS' Jewish audience expect concerning God's kingdom?
   a. that it would be established on earth for eternity
   b. that it was to be experienced in a purely spiritual state
   c. that it would extend beyond the borders of earthly Israel
   d. that its establishment would prepare them for the arrival of their Messiah

2. How does Scripture relate the Son's work of redemption to the Father's will?
   a. as its accomplishment
   b. as its application
   c. as its establishment
   d. as its restoration

· · ·

3. When will believers experience the ability to perfectly obey God's will?

 a. upon their conversion

 b. near the end of their earthly sanctification

 c. never

 d. when they are in resurrected bodies

4. God's preceptive will is defined as: (Choose all that apply.)

 a. his sovereign and mysterious purposes to ordain all that happens

 b. his revealed moral instruction that helps us know his will on earth

 c. his perceived will from the perspective of general revelation

 d. his decretive will when adapted to time and space in history

5. What are we asking when we pray for the Father's will to be done on earth as it is in heaven?

 a. for God to change his decretive will

 b. for God to complete his preceptive will

 c. for God to align our hearts with his revealed will

 d. for God to accomplish his mysterious will among us

6. How is the phrase "on earth as it is in heaven" best understood?

 a. as the fourth petition of the Lord's Prayer

 b. as the culmination of the first three petitions

 c. as the final words of the third petition

 d. as a description of the second and third petitions

Answer Key

Chapter 3 quiz answers are found in the Answer Key.[viii]

Step Nine: Meditate and Pray

All theology should lead us to doxology. The ultimate goal of learning biblical and theological truths is not just to renew our minds, but also to renew our heart affections so that our lives are renewed to the honor of God. Pause now to meditate on and pray about what God is teaching you in his Word. After you pray, consider recording any new insights for application later. Use this prayer outline below if you find it helpful.

- Praise God for his promise to return the fullness of his kingdom on earth forever.
- Confess your failures to align your will on earth with God's will in heaven.
- Thank Jesus for his past, present, and future work to restore God's kingdom on earth.
- Ask the Holy Spirit to renew your mind, heart, and life in greater alignment with God's will.

Here is an example of how you can pray through the petition "Your kingdom come, your will be done, on earth as it is in heaven" in the Lord's Prayer. You can use this as a guide during personal devotions, with your family, in small groups, or with your congregation.

> *Our Father in heaven, we ask you to hallow your*
> *name by causing your kingdom to come and your*
> *will to be done on earth as it is in heaven. Glorify*
> *your name by accomplishing your purpose for*
> *our fallen and broken world—to redeem and*

restore all things through your Son, Jesus Christ,
by the power of your Holy Spirit. Cause your
invisible rule in heaven, where your will is
perfectly accomplished, to become more visible on
earth and in our lives, so that we and all things
may flourish according to your design and give
you the honor that you alone deserve for who
you are and for all you do. Give us the grace and
power to seek first your kingdom and your will in
all things with our whole heart.

Step Ten: Go Deeper as a Lifelong Learner

This step encourages your deeper exploration by using key resources drawn from the chapter article and academic notes to help you grow in your understanding and application of biblical truths, promoting your lifelong learning and continued growth in spiritual maturity.

BIBLE PASSAGES

Gain a deeper understanding and application of the key biblical passages from the chapter article through more in-depth reading, reflection, study, memorization, and meditation.

"Yours, O LORD, is the greatness and the power and the glory and the victory and the majesty, for all that is in the heavens and in the earth is yours. Yours is the kingdom, O LORD, and you are exalted as head above all. Both riches and honor come from you, and you rule over all. In your hand are power and might, and in your hand it is to make great and to give strength to all. And now we thank you, our God, and praise your glorious name." (1 Chron. 29:11–13)

"Now therefore, if you will indeed obey my voice and keep my covenant, you shall be my treasured possession among all peoples, for all the earth is mine; and you shall be to me a kingdom of priests and a holy nation." (Exod. 19:5–6)

"The time is fulfilled, and the kingdom of God is at hand; repent and believe in the gospel." (Mark 1:15)

"But seek first the kingdom of God and his righteousness, and all these things will be added to you." (Matt. 6:33)

"Jesus answered, 'My kingdom is not of this world. If my kingdom were of this world, my servants would have been fighting, that I might not be delivered over to the Jews. But my kingdom is not from the world.'" (John 18:36)

"The whole world lies in the power of the evil one." (1 John 5:19)

"For I have come down from heaven, not to do my own will but the will of him who sent me." (John 6:38)

"I glorified you on earth, having accomplished the work that you gave me to do." (John 17:4)

"He has delivered us from the domain of darkness and transferred us to the kingdom of his beloved Son, in whom we have redemption, the forgiveness of sins." (Col 1:13–14)

"He disarmed the rulers and authorities and put them to open shame, by triumphing over them in him." (Col. 2:15)

"So when they had come together, they asked him, 'Lord, will you at this time restore the kingdom to Israel?' He said to them, 'It is not for you to know times or seasons that the Father has fixed by his own authority. But you will receive power when the Holy Spirit has come upon you, and you will be my witnesses in Jerusalem and in all Judea and Samaria, and to the end of the earth.'" (Acts 1:6–8)

"But you are a chosen race, a royal priesthood, a holy nation, a people for his own possession, that you may proclaim the excellencies of him who called you out of darkness into his marvelous light." (1 Peter 2:9)

"He [Paul] lived there two whole years at his own expense, and welcomed all who came to him, proclaiming the kingdom of God and teaching about the Lord Jesus Christ with all boldness and without hindrance." (Acts 28:30–31)

"Come, you who are blessed by my Father, inherit the kingdom prepared for you from the foundation of the world." (Matt. 25:34)

"Then comes the end, when he delivers the kingdom to God the Father after destroying every rule and every authority and power. For he must reign until he has put all his enemies under his feet. . . . When all things are subjected to him, then the Son himself will also be subjected to him who put all things in subjection under him, that God may be all in all." (1 Cor. 15:24–25, 28)

The Father's will before creation

"Blessed be the God and Father of our Lord Jesus Christ, who has blessed us in Christ with every spiritual blessing in the heavenly places, even as he chose us in him before the foundation of the world, that we should be holy and blameless before him. In love he predestined us for adoption to himself as sons through Jesus Christ, according to the purpose of his will." (Eph. 1:3–5)

The Son's accomplishment of the Father's will in redemption

"[Our adoption is] to the praise of his glorious grace, with which he has blessed us in the Beloved. In him we have redemption through his blood, the forgiveness of our trespasses, according to the riches of his grace, which he lavished upon us, in all wisdom and insight making known to us the mystery of his will, according to his purpose, which he set forth in Christ as a plan for the fullness of time, to unite all things in him, things in heaven and things on earth." (Eph. 1:6–10)

The Spirit's application of the Father's will in sealing believers

"In him we have obtained an inheritance, having been predestined according to the purpose of him who works all things according to the counsel of his will, so that we who were the first to hope in Christ might be to the praise of his glory. In him you also, when you heard the word of truth, the gospel of your salvation, and believed in him, were sealed with the promised Holy Spirit, who is the guarantee of our inheritance until we acquire possession of it, to the praise of his glory." (Eph. 1:11–14)

CATECHISMS

Explore key biblical truths through historic Christian catechisms that offer clear guidance on their meaning and life application.

Westminster Shorter Catechism (QQ. 102–103)

- Q. 102: What do we pray for in the second petition?
- A: In the second petition, which is, Thy kingdom come, we pray that Satan's kingdom may be destroyed; and that the kingdom of grace may be advanced, ourselves and others brought into it, and kept in it; and that the kingdom of glory may be hastened.
- Q. 103: What do we pray for in the third petition?
- A: In the third petition, which is, Thy will be done in earth, as it is in heaven, we pray that God, by his grace, would make us able and willing to know, obey and submit to his will in all things, as the angels do in heaven.

Heidelberg Catechism (QQ. 123–124)

- Q. 123: What does the second petition mean?
- A. "Your kingdom come" means: Rule us by your Word and Spirit in such a way that more and more we submit to you. Preserve your church and make it grow. Destroy the devil's work; destroy every force which revolts against you and every conspiracy against your holy Word. Do this until your kingdom fully comes, when you will be all in all.
- Q. 124: What does the third petition mean?
- A. "Your will be done, on earth as it is in heaven" means: Help us and all people to reject our own wills and to obey your will without any back talk. Your will alone is good. Help us one and all to carry out the work we are called to, as willingly and faithfully as the angels in heaven.

New City Catechism (QQ. 42–43)

- Q. 42: What does the second petition mean?
- A: Your kingdom come means, we are asking God to bring more people to submit to His reign, to destroy evil, and to bring the final establishment of His kingdom when Christ returns in glory.
- Q. 43: What does the third petition mean?
- A: Your will be done on earth as it is in heaven means, we are asking God to make us and others able and willing to obey His will in all things, so that His purposes would be accomplished on earth just as they are perfectly obeyed in heaven.

BOOKS

Expand your understanding of key biblical concepts through selected books that offer more in-depth exploration and practical application.

- Herman Ridderbos, *The Coming of the Kingdom*— Ridderbos makes an in-depth exploration of the kingdom of God, emphasizing how Jesus' life, death, and resurrection initiated God's reign. His scholarly analysis clarifies the meaning of the second petition, "Your kingdom come," and its profound impact on understanding God's rule.

- Graeme Goldsworthy, *Gospel and Kingdom*—This book presents a biblical-theological perspective on the kingdom of God, focusing on how the kingdom is progressively revealed throughout Scripture.

Goldsworthy emphasizes the kingdom's fulfillment in Christ.

- Thomas Watson, *All Things for Good*—Watson explores how God's will always works for the ultimate good of his people, aligning perfectly with his kingdom purposes. He draws on Romans 8:28 to show how God's providence operates in every detail of the believer's life, whether good or bad, ultimately for their good and for his glory.

HYMNS

Allow these biblical truths to lead you to praise and worship God with prayers and hymns that honor God for who he is and what he does.

- "Jesus Shall Reign Where'er the Sun," by Isaac Watts—A classic hymn that vividly reflects the global spread of the Father's rule and reign (his kingdom) through his Son, depicting the universal and eternal reign of Christ extending to every corner of the earth, "where'er the sun doth its successive journeys run."

- "All Hail the Power of Jesus' Name," by Edward Perronet—A triumphant hymn that celebrates the universal power and authority of Christ, calling all creation to bow before him to bring honor to his name. This hymn reflects the Father's kingdom advancing through his Son as all heavenly and earthly beings fall before him in worship.

- "Crown Him with Many Crowns," by Matthew Bridges and Godfrey Thring—A majestic hymn that exalts Christ's eternal kingship, celebrating his victory and reign. It reflects God's magnificent rule as Christ, the "Lamb upon his throne," who is crowned and glorified by all of creation for who he is and what he's done.

MANWARD PETITIONS

4

OUR DAILY BREAD

Step One: Read the Introduction

J esus knew that our anxiety about not having what we need in life could easily divert us from our mission of honoring the Father's name by advancing his kingdom and will on earth. For us to overcome this temptation and flourish in our mission, Jesus taught us to pray, "Give us this day our daily bread" (Matt. 6:11).

In the petition for daily bread, Jesus teaches us how to trust in our heavenly Father to give us what is necessary each day to carry out his mission. Our continual need for physical nourishment reminds us that we continually need our Father's provision for all things necessary in life and that our greatest need is ultimately met by the Father's giving us himself by his Holy Spirit.

By teaching us how to ask for our daily bread, Jesus means for us to learn to increase our daily dependence on our heavenly Father when tempted in both poverty and riches. For Jesus' followers to honor the Father's name and fulfill his kingdom mission, they must overcome these dangerous temptations by learning to trust in the Father's protection to provide for them.

Ultimately, Jesus' purpose in instructing us to ask our Father for our necessary daily provisions in life is not to teach us that we will always receive what we think is necessary, but to teach us to be obedient and to trust that what we receive from our heavenly Father is truly best and necessary to do his will.

In this chapter, we will learn to petition God for our daily needs, protection, and obedience in faith.

Step Two: Review the Learning Goals

Learning Goals

In this chapter, you will be equipped to:

- Pray to the Father for our daily bread to fulfill our mission and to trust him more deeply.
- Pray for our protection from temptations of poverty and riches.
- Pray for what we need, knowing that it may differ from what we want.
- Pray that our suffering would drive us to find our strength in Christ.

Step Three: Review the Key Ideas

Key Ideas

In this chapter, these are the key ideas:

- We ask for our daily bread to help us overcome temptation and flourish in our mission.
- We ask for our daily bread for protection from temptations of poverty and riches.

- When we ask for our daily provisions, we will not always receive what we want, but we will always receive exactly what we need.
- When we do not receive what we ask God for, we find a strength beyond ourselves.

Step Four: Answer the Reflection Questions

Take a moment before reading the chapter article to reflect on these questions. They'll help you connect your beliefs, desires, and practices with the topics ahead, allowing for deeper engagement and more practical application to your life and ministry.

1. What specifically do you request when you pray: "Give us ... our daily bread"?
2. How do you respond when God does not give you what you request?

Step Five: Read the Chapter Article with Academic Notes

There are two sets of petitions in the Lord's Prayer. The first set is vertical, focusing on God, in which we ask for our Father's name to be hallowed, for his kingdom to come, and for his will to be done on earth as it is in heaven. The second set includes horizontal requests, in which we ask our Father for our daily bread, for our forgiveness, and for our deliverance.[1]

It's important to understand how these two sets of petitions

---

1. The first petitions repeat the pronoun "your" three times: (1) "hallowed be *your* name," (2) "*Your* kingdom come," and (3) "*your* will be done." The second petitions include eight personal pronouns in three statements: (1) "Give *us* this day *our* daily bread," (2) "forgive *us* *our* debts, as *we* also have forgiven *our* debtors," and (3) "lead *us* not into temptation, but deliver *us* from evil" (Matt. 6:9–13).

are interconnected. The reason we pray for our daily bread, forgiveness, and deliverance is so that we can honor our Father's name by advancing his kingdom and carrying out his will on earth as it is in heaven. Jesus taught that one of the most dangerous temptations that his followers face is having an inordinate focus on "treasures on earth" and "money" instead of "treasures in heaven" and "God" (Matt. 6:19–24). He refers to these temptations as the "cares [anxieties] of the world" and the "deceitfulness of riches" that result in people's "fall[ing] away" and becoming "unfruitful" (13:18–22). To help us overcome the temptation to let our anxiety about what we think we need in life divert us from flourishing in our mission, Jesus instructs us to pray to our heavenly Father, "Give us this day our daily bread."

PRAYING for Our Needs

The New Testament Greek word translated "bread" (ἄρτον) in Matthew 6:11 can refer both to the physical bread we eat and to all the basic provisions of life we need.[2] The Greek adjective (ἐπιούσιον) used to describe the bread is difficult to translate and is not used in any other place in the New Testament except

2. Martin Luther writes: "Question: What is meant by 'daily bread'? Answer: All that belongs to the wants and support of the body, such as meat, drink, clothing, shoes, house, home, land, cattle, money, goods, a pious spouse, pious children, pious servants, pious and faithful rulers, good government, good weather, peace, health, order, honor, good friends, trusty neighbors and the like." Then he comments: "If you speak of, and pray for, daily bread, you pray for everything that is necessary in order to have and enjoy the same, and also against everything which interferes with it. Therefore, you must enlarge your thoughts and extend them afar, not only to the oven or the flour-barrel, but to the distant field and the entire land, which bears and brings to us daily bread and every sort of sustenance. For if God did not cause it to grow, and bless and preserve it in the field, we could never take bread from the oven or have any to set upon the table." Martin Luther, *The Book of Concord: The Confessions of the Evangelical Lutheran Church*, ed. Robert Kolb and Timothy J. Wengert, trans. Charles Arand et al. (Fortress Press, 2000), The Fourth Petition, 402–3, 501.

in Luke's record of the Lord's Prayer in Luke 11:2–4.[3] It can be translated "daily," but its fuller meaning is most likely conveyed by the word "necessary."

Jesus is not just teaching us to ask our heavenly Father to give us all the provisions that are necessary to sustain our physical lives each day. His broader purpose is to teach us how to trust in our heavenly Father to give us what is *necessary* each day to carry out his mission—with or without the daily provisions that we may *think* are necessary.

Luke's account of Jesus teaching the Lord's Prayer is immediately followed by Jesus' teaching that we should be persistent in our prayers, always bringing our needs to God as our heavenly Father with the persistent confidence of his beloved children that he will always hear and answer our prayers. Jesus assures us:

> I tell you, ask, and it will be given to you; seek, and you will find; knock, and it will be opened to you. For everyone who asks receives, and the one who seeks finds, and to the one who knocks it will be opened. What father among you, if his son asks for a fish, will instead of a fish give him a serpent; or if he asks for an egg, will give him a scorpion? (Luke 11:9–12)

Then Jesus teaches that our heavenly Father's greatest answer to our prayers is not necessarily receiving what we ask him to give us, but receiving the far superior gift of himself in the Holy Spirit. "If you then, who are evil, know how to give good gifts to your children, how much more will the heavenly Father give *the Holy Spirit* to those who ask him!" (Luke 11:13).[4]

---

3. ἐπιούσιον may be the best equivalent Greek word for the unknown Aramaic word that Jesus used.
4. In Matthew's account, Jesus includes the son's request for bread and the Father's promise to "give good things": "Or which one of you, *if his son asks him for bread, will give him a stone? Or if he asks for a fish, will give him a serpent? If*

Our continual need for physical nourishment should remind us of our continual need for our Father's provision of not just our food, but also all other things we need for life. We should always be asking our heavenly Father to give us *good gifts*, such as food, but all the while knowing that the ultimate gift that our Father promises us, which meets our greatest need, is himself by his Holy Spirit.

PRAYING for Our Protection

Similar to the way in which the prayer's vertical petitions for the Father's name, kingdom, and will are found in the Old Testament,[5] we also find the horizontal petitions in the Old Testament.[6]

For example, in Jesus' instruction for us to pray for "our daily bread," he is echoing an ancient Jewish prayer: "feed me

---

you then, who are evil, know how to give good gifts to your children, how much more will your Father who is in heaven give *good things* to those who ask him!" (Matt. 7:9–11).

5. Old Testament scholar Rick Byargeon shows the striking similarity between the Jewish synagogue prayer *Qaddish* and the Lord's Prayer. "The *Qaddish* begins with the phrase 'Exalted and hallowed be his great name,' which parallels 'hallowed be your name' in Matthew 6:9. The second expression shared between the two prayers is related to the coming kingdom. The *Qaddish* states: 'May he establish his kingdom in your lifetime.' This parallels the expression, 'your kingdom come' in Matthew 6:10." Rick W. Byargeon, "Echoes of Wisdom in the Lord's Prayer (Matt 6:9–13)," *Journal of the Evangelical Theological Society* 41, no. 3 (September 1998): 354.

6. One of the most prominent prayers of Judaism, called "The Prayer" (*hattepilla*), was compiled and standardized by Gamaliel as "Eighteen Benedictions" at Jamnia after the destruction of the temple near the end of the first century. Benediction 9 seems to have similar content to "Give us this day our daily bread." "Bless, O Lord our God, this year for us, and let it be good in all the varieties of its produce. Hasten the year of our redemptive end. Grant dew and rain upon the face of the earth, and satiate the world out of the treasuries of Your goodness; and grant a blessing to the work of our hands." Gamaliel, "Eighteen Benedictions," Benediction 9, in *The Jewish Prayer Book*, compiled and standardized at Jamnia, late 1st century.

with the food that is *needful* for me" (Prov. 30:8). This ancient "wisdom prayer" was probably one of the first-century Jewish synagogue prayers used in corporate worship.[7]

The book of Proverbs teaches that true wisdom is achieved by honoring God and submitting to his will in all of life's circumstances (Prov. 1:7). And the truly wise person knows how to honor God and obey his will when facing the unique temptations that come from poverty and riches. To help us be wise when asking God to provide us with what is truly necessary in this life, he instructs us, in Proverbs 30:8–9, to ask him for protection from both kinds of temptations:

> Give me neither poverty nor riches; feed me with the food that is needful for me, lest I be full and deny you and say, "Who is the LORD?" or lest I be poor and steal and profane the name of my God.

There is a strong echo from the Proverbs 30 petition "feed me with the food that is needful for me" in the Lord's Prayer petition "Give us this day our daily [needful] bread." A shared ultimate prayer for honoring God's name is also found in both prayers. In Proverbs 30:9, the request for needful food is made so that the person praying does not "profane the name of my God." And in the Lord's Prayer, the request for daily bread is the first of several petitions offered so that the Father's name will be hallowed (not profaned).

For Jesus' followers to honor the Father's name and fulfill

---

7. The prayers in Proverbs 30 address the dangers of pride and arrogance and include examples of when a slave "becomes king" and when a fool "*is filled with food*" (Prov. 30:22). One of the strongest parallels between Proverbs 30 and the Lord's Prayer is found in Proverbs 30:8, in which the Hebrew text הַטְרִיפֵנִי לֶחֶם (חֻקִּי) conveys the meaning "Let me eat my appointed/apportioned bread." The Hebrew word (חֻקִּי) used to describe the bread reflects the idea of a specific allotment of bread that is appointed and sufficient for a prescribed amount of time—reflected in the petition "Give us this day *our daily bread.*"

his kingdom mission, they must overcome these dangerous temptations of poverty and riches by learning how to trust in their heavenly Father to give them everything that is necessary *each day* to carry out his mission.

Jesus' primary purpose in giving us this petition is to increase our daily dependence on our heavenly Father—especially when we're facing the kinds of temptations brought about by either poverty or riches—temptations that can easily divert us from carrying out the Father's will.

Jesus knew firsthand the power of these temptations. Before he was tempted by the devil in the wilderness, he ate nothing for forty days. Matthew notes, "After fasting forty days and forty nights, *he was hungry*" (Matt. 4:2).

We can be confident that during his time in the wilderness, Jesus was asking his Father to give him what he needed each day to carry out his will. And after forty days without food, Jesus was approaching the limits of having what is necessary to stay alive physically.

Satan seized this vulnerable moment to tempt Jesus to stop trusting in his Father to provide what he needed and start trusting in his own ability by turning stones into bread. Satan said, "If you are the Son of God, command these stones to become loaves of bread" (Matt. 4:3).[8]

Jesus resisted this temptation and quoted a passage from Deuteronomy 8, "It is written, 'Man shall not live by bread alone, but by every word that comes from the mouth of God'" (Matt. 4:4). He told Satan that what would ultimately sustain his life was not physical bread but his Father's will. So Jesus

---

8. Luther writes: "But this petition [for daily bread] is especially directed against our chief enemy, the devil. For all his thought and desire is occupied with depriving us of all that we have from God and hindering us in its enjoyment. . . . He is sorry that anyone has a morsel of bread from God and eats the same in peace." *Book of Concord*, The Fourth Petition, 502.

continued trusting in his Father's word to provide him with everything he needed to do his will.[9]

PRAYING for Our Obedience

When his disciples became concerned that Jesus had not eaten in a while, they urged him to eat. Jesus responded by saying, "I have food to eat that you do not know about." So the disciples asked one another, "Has anyone brought him something to eat?" Jesus then replied, "My food is to do the will of him who sent me and to accomplish his work" (John 4:31–34).

Jesus is teaching that our lives are ultimately sustained or lost not by things like physical food, but by our Father's will. So the time we're alive on earth is ultimately determined not by the number of physical provisions we have but by how long it takes us to accomplish our Father's will for our lives.

Trusting in his heavenly Father to provide for all his daily needs was a hallmark of Jesus' brief life and ministry. When a religious leader showed an interest in following Jesus, he told

---

9. The passage that Jesus quotes in Deuteronomy 8 is from Moses' message to the people of Israel whom God taught this same lesson about trusting him for their daily needs during their forty years in the wilderness. To help the Israelites learn how to trust in him to care for them as they carried out his will, God provided for them daily only enough bread (*manna*) to sustain them for that one day. This bread could not be stockpiled to provide for their needs in the future. God did not do this to punish Israel, but as a form of loving discipline, so that his people would learn how to trust in him to always provide for their needs as they kept their primary focus on him and on carrying out his will on earth. Moses exhorts them to remember this valuable lesson: "*He humbled you and let you hunger and fed you with manna . . . , that he might make you know that man does not live by bread alone, but man lives by every word that comes from the mouth of the Lord.* Your clothing did not wear out on you and your foot did not swell these forty years. Know then in your heart that, as a man disciplines his son, the Lord your God disciplines you" (Deut. 8:3–5). Sadly, the people of Israel failed this test during their forty years in the wilderness, but Jesus, the *True Israel*, passed this test, not only in his forty days of temptation in the wilderness, but also when he faced the same daily temptations throughout his life.

the leader, "Foxes have holes, and birds of the air have nests, but the Son of Man has nowhere to lay his head" (Matt. 8:20). Following Jesus requires following his example of trusting in our heavenly Father to give us everything we need *each day* to carry out his mission.

Our Father did not always give Jesus the daily physical care and comfort that he longed for and asked for. This does not mean that his Father stopped loving him—although it sometimes felt like it. Instead, Jesus learned that if the Father withheld what he thought he needed, it was because he did not need it to carry out his Father's will. So it was sometimes actually better for Jesus not to have his physical needs met.

Through his suffering, the One who said, "My food is to do the will of him who sent me and to accomplish his work" (John 4:34), received the higher blessing of learning greater levels of obedience to his Father's will. "Although he was a son, he learned obedience through what he suffered. And being made perfect, he became the source of eternal salvation to all who obey him" (Heb. 5:8–9).

Therefore, Jesus' purpose in instructing us to ask our Father for our necessary daily provisions in life is not to teach us that we will always receive what we think is necessary, but to teach us that what we receive from our heavenly Father is truly best and necessary for us to do his will.

The same Jesus who teaches his followers not to be anxious about having the necessities of life, urging, "But seek first the kingdom of God and his righteousness, *and all these things will be added to you*" (Matt. 6:33), also warns, "You will be delivered up even by parents and brothers and relatives and friends, and some of you they will put to death" (Luke 21:16). Jesus doesn't tell us how they will be put to death, but we know that many of his followers were tortured or died of hunger.

Immediately after Jesus describes the horrific suffering that his followers might experience, he makes a promise to them,

"But not a hair of your head will perish" (Luke 21:18), showing that this promise, like his many others, does not include a promise of no physical harm.

The apostle Paul gives us a long list of horrible physical circumstances he faced in his life and ministry, including "imprisonments," "countless beatings" from which he almost died, and a host of other dangerous situations in which he experienced "many a sleepless night, *in hunger and thirst, often without food, in cold and exposure*" (2 Cor. 11:23–27).

The same Paul who believed Jesus' promise that when he suffered "not a hair of [his] head will perish" was most likely beheaded in prison for his faith.[10] In all these difficult circumstances, when God did not give Paul the daily provisions and comfort he longed for and asked for, Paul learned that God was not abandoning him, but was giving him something far better that he needed much more—the soul-nourishing Bread of Life in Jesus Christ. As a result, Paul writes:

> I know how to be brought low, and I know how to abound. In any and every circumstance, I have learned the secret of facing plenty and hunger, abundance and need. I can do all things through him who strengthens me. (Phil. 4:12–13)

CONCLUSION

Sometimes our heavenly Father answers our prayer for our necessary provisions in life by giving us abundance. Other

10. In his last letter before his death, Paul writes: "For I am already being poured out as a drink offering, and the time of my departure has come. I have fought the good fight, I have finished the race, I have kept the faith. Henceforth there is laid up for me the crown of righteousness, which the Lord, the righteous judge, will award to me on that day, and not only to me but also to all who have loved his appearing" (2 Tim. 4:6–8).

times he answers our prayer by giving us a lack of physical provisions and a painful experience of suffering that increases our trust in him and our obedience to his will.

The apostle Peter teaches that we're all called to follow Jesus in his suffering: "For *to this you have been called*, because Christ also suffered for you, leaving you an example, so that you might follow in his steps" (1 Peter 2:21). Paul writes, "For it has been granted to you that for the sake of Christ you should not only believe in him but also suffer for his sake" (Phil. 1:29).

Not having the things that we think we need in life can sometimes be a good thing. Our physical suffering and hunger heighten our sense of need and drive us to our heavenly Father to find in him a strength beyond ourselves. Suffering is not something that followers of Jesus should be avoiding at all costs. If Jesus learned obedience to the Father's will through the things he suffered, are his followers above their Master?

Therefore, Jesus instructs us that in any and every circumstance, when facing plenty or hunger, we are to keep asking our heavenly Father to give us each day exactly what we need to honor his name and carry out his will—and then trust in him and his promise to give us exactly what we need.[11]

Step Six: Answer the Review Questions with Answer Key

Try to answer the Review Questions below on your own before you refer to the Answer Key in the back of the book.

1. What is Jesus' broader purpose in teaching you to pray for our daily bread?[i]

---

11. J. I. Packer writes: "Now comes the real test of faith. You, the Christian, have (I assume) prayed for today's bread. Will you now believe that what comes to you, much or little, is God's answer, according to the promise of Matthew 6:33? And will you on that basis be content with it, and grateful for it? Over to you." J. I. Packer, *Growing in Christ* (Crossway, 1994), 190.

2. How does Jesus' teaching on persistence in prayer, as recorded in Luke, help you understand why you should keep asking for daily bread?[ii]

3. What are the temptations from which you need protection?[iii]

4. Why do you not always receive what you think is necessary when you pray for daily bread?[iv]

Step Seven: Answer the Discussion Questions with Sample Answers

Reflect on these questions either individually or in a group. They are intended to renew your understanding, stir your heart's desires, and deepen your love for God and others. Try to answer each question on your own before consulting the sample answers in the Answer Key.

1. Mind for Truth: How does asking God for daily provision help you resist specific temptations you face today?[v]

2. Heart for God: What concerns or needs tempt you to illegitimately lean on your own understanding?[vi]

3. Life for Ministry: Other than your prayers, what do you think will change if you live according to this petition?[vii]

Step Eight: Take the Review Quiz with Answer Key

This quiz is designed to help you recall and apply key concepts you're learning, increasing your understanding of these concepts for practical application in life and ministry. Try to answer each question on your own before you refer to the Answer Key.

. . .

1. What do the words *daily bread* convey in the Lord's Prayer? (Choose all that apply.)
   a. our necessary needs
   b. our everyday food
   c. our daily spiritual needs

2. What is the superior gift in praying for our daily bread?
   a. the things that we ask for
   b. the gift of God in the Holy Spirit
   c. the things that we never knew we needed
   d. the food that we eat every day

3. What are the two unique temptations shown to us in Proverbs 30?
   a. anger and lust
   b. poverty and covetousness
   c. riches and greed
   d. poverty and riches

4. WHAT IS JESUS' primary purpose in teaching us to pray for our daily bread? (Choose all that apply.)
   a. to help us resist Satan's deceitfulness
   b. to give us a means to ask for our earthly needs
   c. to increase our daily dependence on our heavenly Father
   d. to provide us with wisdom from Proverbs

5. Why did our heavenly Father not always give Jesus the daily physical care and comfort that he desired and requested? (Choose all that apply.)
   a. He knew that Jesus did not need it to carry out his will.

b. He knew that it was better for Jesus not to have his physical needs met.

c. He wanted Jesus to experience suffering.

6. "Not having what we think we need and pray to have can sometimes be good for us."
   a. true
   b. false

Answer Key

Chapter 4 quiz answers are found in the Answer Key.[viii]

Step Nine: Meditate and Pray

All theology should lead us to doxology. The ultimate goal of learning biblical and theological truths is not just to renew our minds, but also to renew our heart affections so that our lives are renewed to the honor of God. Pause now to meditate on and pray about what God is teaching you in his Word. After you pray, consider recording any new insights for application later. Use this prayer outline below if you find it helpful.

- Praise God that he knows all your needs before you even pray for them.
- Confess how you often confuse your needs with your wants and fall prey to the temptations of poverty and riches.
- Thank Jesus for his example of trusting that his Father (and your Father) will always provide what is truly best for you to do his will.
- Ask the Holy Spirit to heighten your sense of need

and reveal Jesus to you in a way that drives you to experience more of our heavenly Father's love.

Here is an example of how you can pray through the petition "Give us this day our daily bread" in the Lord's Prayer. You can use this as a guide during personal devotions, with your family, in small groups, or with your congregation.

> *Our Father in heaven, we come before you, asking for our daily bread, trusting in your perfect provision for all our physical and spiritual needs. Provide us with everything necessary to fulfill your will—whether in abundance or in scarcity —trusting that each day's bread comes from your loving hand. Guard us from the temptation to rely on material security and teach us to depend fully on you, knowing that you care for us in every circumstance. As we ask for our daily bread, grant us contentment with whatever you provide, whether we are in plenty or in want. Remind us that our true sustenance comes from you and your perfect will. In both our need and abundance, strengthen our hearts to trust in your promises. Remind us that you will always give us exactly what we need to honor your name, advance your kingdom, and carry out your will. Grant us grace this day to depend fully on you and to be generous with others, reflecting your love and care in all that we do.*

Step Ten: Go Deeper as a Lifelong Learner

This step encourages your deeper exploration by using key resources drawn from the chapter article and academic notes to help you grow in your understanding and application of biblical truths, promoting your lifelong learning and continued growth in spiritual maturity.

BIBLE PASSAGES

Gain a deeper understanding and application of the key biblical passages from the chapter article through more in-depth reading, reflection, study, memorization, and meditation.

"Give me neither poverty nor riches; feed me with the food that is needful for me, lest I be full and deny you and say, "Who is the LORD?" or lest I be poor and steal and profane the name of my God." (Prov. 30:8–9)

"Then Jesus was led up by the Spirit into the wilderness to be tempted by the devil. And after fasting forty days and forty nights, he was hungry. And the tempter came and said to him, 'If you are the Son of God, command these stones to become loaves of bread.' But he answered,' It is written, "Man shall not live by bread alone, but by every word that comes from the mouth of God.""" (Matt. 4: 1–4)

"Do not lay up for yourselves treasures on earth, where moth and rust destroy and where thieves break in and steal, but lay up for yourselves treasures in heaven, where neither moth nor rust destroys and where thieves do not break in and steal. For where your treasure is, there your heart will be also. The eye is the lamp of the body. So, if your eye is healthy, your whole body will be full of light, but if your eye is bad, your whole body will be full of darkness. If then the light in you is darkness, how great is the darkness! No one can serve two masters, for either he will hate the one and love the other, or he will be devoted to the one and despise the other. You cannot serve God and money." (Matt. 6:19–24)

"But seek first the kingdom of God and his righteousness, and all these things will be added to you." (Matt. 6:33)

"And a scribe came up and said to him, 'Teacher, I will follow you wherever you go.' And Jesus said to him, 'Foxes have holes, and birds of the air have nests, but the Son of Man has nowhere to lay his head.'" (Matt. 8:19–20)

"I tell you, ask, and it will be given to you; seek, and you will find; knock, and it will be opened to you. For everyone who asks receives, and the one who seeks finds, and to the one who knocks it will be opened. What father among you, if his son asks for a fish, will instead of a fish give him a serpent; or if he asks for an egg, will give him a scorpion? If you then, who are evil, know how to give good gifts to your children, how much more will the heavenly Father give the Holy Spirit to those who ask him!" (Luke 11:9–13)

"You will be delivered up even by parents and brothers and relatives and friends, and some of you they will put to death. You will be hated by all for my name's sake. But not a hair of your head will perish. By your endurance you will gain your lives." (Luke 21:16–19)

"Meanwhile the disciples were urging him, saying, 'Rabbi, eat.' But he said to them, 'I have food to eat that you do not know about.'" (John 4:31–32)

"Although he was a son, he learned obedience through what he suffered. And being made perfect, he became the source of eternal salvation to all who obey him." (Heb. 5:8–9)

"For to this you have been called, because Christ also suffered for you, leaving you an example, so that you might follow in his steps." (1 Peter 2:21)

"For it has been granted to you that for the sake of Christ you should not only believe in him but also suffer for his sake." (Phil. 1:29)

"Not that I am speaking of being in need, for I have learned in whatever situation I am to be content. I know how to be brought low, and I know how to abound. In any and every circumstance, I have learned the secret of facing plenty and hunger, abundance and need. I can do all things through him who strengthens me." (Phil. 4:11–13)

CATECHISMS

Explore key biblical truths through historic Christian catechisms that offer clear guidance on their meaning and life application.

Westminster Shorter Catechism (Q. 104)

- Q. 104: What do we pray for in the fourth petition?
- A: In the fourth petition, which is, *Give us this day our daily bread*, we pray that of God's free gift we may receive a competent portion of the good things of this life, and enjoy his blessing with them.

Westminster Larger Catechism (Q. 193)

- Q. 193: What do we pray for in the fourth petition?

- A. In the fourth petition (which is, *Give us this day our daily bread*), acknowledging that in Adam, and by our own sin, we have forfeited our right to all the outward blessings of this life, and deserve to be wholly deprived of them by God, and to have them cursed to us in the use of them; and that neither they of themselves are able to sustain us, nor we to merit, or by our own industry to procure them; but prone to desire, get, and use them unlawfully: we pray for ourselves and others, that both they and we, waiting upon the providence of God from day to day in the use of lawful means, may, of his free gift, and as to his fatherly wisdom shall seem best, enjoy a competent portion of them; and have the same continued and blessed unto us in our holy and comfortable use of them, and contentment in them; and be kept from all things that are contrary to our temporal support and comfort.

Heidelberg Catechism (Q. 125)

- Q. 125: What does the fourth petition mean?
- A. "Give us this day our daily bread" means: Do take care of all our physical needs so that we come to know that you are the only source of everything good, and that neither our work and worry nor your gifts can do us any good without your blessing. And so help us to give up our trust in creatures and trust in you alone.

BOOKS

Expand your understanding of key biblical concepts

through selected books that offer more in-depth exploration
and practical application.

- Jeremiah Burroughs, *The Rare Jewel of Christian
  Contentment*—Burroughs addresses the heart of
  contentment, an essential concept linked to asking
  God for daily bread. This book guides readers in
  learning how to find satisfaction in God's provision,
  regardless of circumstances.

- Thomas Watson, *The Art of Divine Contentment*—
  Watson's classic work centers on contentment, as
  taught in Philippians 4:11, guiding readers to find
  satisfaction in God's daily provision, showing that
  true peace comes from trusting his sovereignty,
  regardless of life's circumstances.

- Timothy Keller, *Counterfeit Gods: The Empty Promises
  of Money, Sex, and Power, and the Only Hope That
  Matters*—Keller addresses modern idols that fuel
  our discontentment with alluring but empty
  promises and that replace our dependence on God,
  who alone can satisfy our deepest needs.

~

HYMNS

Allow these biblical truths to lead you to praise and
worship God with prayers and hymns that honor God for who
he is and what he does.

- "Our God, Our Help in Ages Past," by Isaac Watts—
  Watts draws from Psalm 90, celebrating God's
  steadfast protection, promised provision, and tender

care for his people across all generations, assuring believers of his unchanging faithfulness to provide what they need.

- "Guide Me, O Thou Great Jehovah," by William Williams—Drawing from the Israelites' wilderness journey, this hymn calls upon God for his daily provision. The line "Bread of heaven, feed me now and evermore" reflects a deep reliance on God's faithful care.

- "Great Is Thy Faithfulness," by Thomas Chisholm—Inspired by Lamentations 3:22–23, this hymn praises God for his unchanging faithfulness and his promised daily provision, reassuring believers that God's steadfast care meets every need, morning by morning.

5

OUR FORGIVENESS

Step One: Read the Introduction

After Jesus teaches us to pray for our necessary physical provisions, he instructs us to pray for God to forgive our sins as we forgive those who sin against us.

Jesus teaches that *we owe God a perfect love for him and others.* But since we cannot love and have not loved God and others perfectly, we owe God an enormous debt that we cannot pay. As a result, we are all guilty before God and under his just condemnation. Because of God's perfect holiness, he must punish evil and sin.

The Scriptures teach that God graciously provides *for us* in Jesus Christ what he justly demands *of us* in his law. Forgiving the sins of all who have faith in Jesus is a just thing for God to do because Jesus fully satisfied all the demands of God's holy justice through his sinless life and sacrificial death in our place.

Jesus also teaches that it is *necessary* for us to forgive others in order to receive our forgiveness from God. But our forgiveness of others is not the *cause* of our forgiveness; it is the *evidence* that we are forgiven. God does not forgive us *because we forgive others.* God forgives us because Jesus died for us. We reveal our forgiveness by forgiving others.

In this chapter, we will learn to ask God to forgive our sins as we forgive those who sin against us.

Step Two: Review the Learning Goals

Learning Goals

In this chapter, you will be equipped to:

- Pray with understanding that the nature of our sin is debt and that God's holiness requires sin's punishment.
- Pray with gratitude that Christ satisfied God's just demands.
- Pray with thankfulness for God's justice in forgiving us.
- Pray in ongoing repentance and faith for forgiveness of our debts and that our forgiveness would be revealed by our forgiving of others.

Step Three: Review the Key Ideas

Key Ideas

In this chapter, these are the key ideas:

- God cannot overlook our disobedience because of his perfect holiness.
- God provides for us in Jesus Christ what he demands of us in his law.
- God justly forgives us by Christ's sacrificial, substitutionary life and death.

- Our ongoing repentant prayers and forgiveness of others are evidence of our forgiveness in Christ.

Step Four: Answer the Reflection Questions

Take a moment before reading the chapter article to reflect on these questions. They'll help you connect your beliefs, desires, and practices with the topics ahead, allowing for deeper engagement and more practical application to your life and ministry.

1. What do you think forgiving a debt means?
2. Why do you think it is necessary for us to forgive others?

Step Five: Read the Chapter Article with Academic Notes

We must have God's forgiveness to experience the fullness of his unfolding purposes for our lives. After Jesus teaches us to pray for our necessary physical provisions, he instructs us to pray, "Forgive us our debts, as we also have forgiven our debtors" (Matt. 6:12).

The Greek word translated "forgive" (ἀφίημι) conveys the idea of letting something go, giving something up, or releasing something. The word translated "debts" (ὀφείλημα) refers to something that someone owes, that which is legally required.

Therefore, to forgive a debt means to release it by considering it to be no longer owed or required. In the rabbinic teachings of the first century and the parables of Jesus, a person's failure to obey God is like a debt someone owes to a king, landowner, or someone else.[1]

---

1. Jesus taught a parable about a servant who could not repay a large debt he owed a king, so he pleaded for mercy and the king forgave his debt. But later

. . .

OUR DEBTS

Jesus uses monetary debt as a metaphor of the debt we owe to God because of our failure to obey his will. God's will is for us to honor him by loving him and doing what he commands. When we disobey God's will by doing something he commands us not to do (sin of commission) or by not doing what he commands us to do (sin of omission), we are failing to fulfill our obligations to God and accumulating a great debt owed to him.[2]

Jesus uses other words and metaphors to help us understand the nature of sin.[3] But the specific metaphor that Jesus gives us in this second horizontal petition is that of unpaid debts (ὀφείλημα) we owe to God because of our many failures to obey his will.

Since God's moral law, revealed especially in the Ten Commandments, requires our perfect obedience, Jesus claims: "You therefore must be *perfect*, as your heavenly Father is

---

the ungrateful servant did not forgive a much smaller debt to someone who owed him (Matt.18:21–35). Jesus also taught about a lender who forgave two debtors, one with a large debt and the other with a small one. The debtor with the large debt loved the lender more than the one with the smaller one (Luke 7:41–50).

2. The Westminster catechisms define *sin* as "any want of conformity unto, or transgression of, any law of God" (Larger Catechism Q. 24). But the Scriptures present sin as more than violating a known law of God. The *Anglican Book of Common Prayer* declares, "Sin is that which we have done, or left undone, known and unknown, and includes any intimation or embodiment of not loving God with our whole heart or not loving our neighbor as ourselves."

3. Immediately after giving us the petitions of the Lord's Prayer, Jesus uses another Greek word for "sin," translated "trespasses" (παραπτώματα), that conveys the picture of someone's crossing over a forbidden line or border (Matt. 6:14–15). In Luke's account of the Lord's Prayer, Jesus uses a Greek word translated "sins" (ἁμαρτίας) that portrays someone as missing a target or mark (Luke 11:4). And later in the Sermon on the Mount, he uses a Greek word for "sin," translated "lawlessness" (ἀνομία), describing someone's failing to observe a law (Matt. 7:23).

perfect" (Matt. 5:48). Jesus teaches that *we owe God a perfect love for him and others.*

But since we cannot love and have not loved God and others perfectly, the Scriptures teach that we owe God an enormous debt that we cannot pay. As a result, we're all guilty before God and under his just condemnation.

GOD'S FORGIVENESS of Our Debts

The great dilemma presented to us in Scripture is how a holy and just God can forgive our sins without being unjust. God's holy justice requires him to actively oppose all evil. God promises to punish sin. He "will by no means clear the guilty" (Ex. 34:7).

The Bible teaches that there are certain things God cannot do. For example, God cannot lie, God cannot change his mind, and God cannot break a promise.[4] And because of God's perfect holiness, he cannot overlook evil and sin. He must punish it, or he would be unjust.

God could create the world out of nothing, by the power of his word, but God cannot forgive us by overlooking our sin and just "deciding to forgive us" as a political leader can decide to grant amnesty and pardon a criminal. This is because God's righteous nature demands that sin be punished with the full outpouring of his wrath.[5] God's mercy is infinite, but so is his

---

4. "God is not man, that he should lie, or a son of man, that he should change his mind. Has he said, and will he not do it? Or has he spoken, and will he not fulfill it?" (Num. 23:19). "It is impossible for God to lie" (Heb. 6:18).

5. Leon Morris writes: "Unpalatable though it may be, our sins, my sins, are the object of God's wrath. We must realize that every sin is displeasing to God and that unless something is done about the evil we have committed, we face ultimately nothing less than the divine anger." Leon Morris, *Apostolic Preaching of the Cross* (Eerdmans, 1955), 175.

justice, so it's with deep sorrow that he must punish sin[6] (James 2:10; 1 Peter 1:16–17).

The Scriptures teach that God graciously provides *for us* in Jesus Christ what he justly demands *of us* in his law. Through Jesus' sinless life and sacrificial death on the cross in our place, he perfectly obeyed all of God's laws *for us* so that he could fully satisfy all of God's just demands *of us*. Justification is God's astonishing declaration that all who are in Christ by faith are considered by him to be perfectly righteous (just) based on Jesus' blood and righteousness (Rom. 3:21–25; Gal. 2:16).[7]

When we believe in Christ, a *great exchange* takes place in the heavenly court. "For our sake he [God] made him [Christ] to be sin who knew no sin, so that in him we might become the righteousness of God" (2 Cor. 5:21). God treated Jesus like a sinner so that he could treat us like Jesus. God satisfied his own

---

6. This presents us with one of the most profound mysteries and questions in the universe. Now that sin has entered the world, how can God be both fully just and fully merciful? Horatius Bonar writes: "God is a Father; but He is no less a Judge. Shall the Judge give way to the Father, or the Father give way to the Judge? God loves the sinner; but He hates the sin. Shall He sink His love to the sinner in His hatred of the sin, or His hatred of the sin in His love to the sinner? . . . Which is the more unchangeable and irreversible, the vow of pity or the oath of justice? . . . Law and love must be reconciled. . . . The one cannot give way to the other. Both must stand, else the pillars of the universe will be shaken." Horatius Bonar, *The Everlasting Righteousness* (Banner of Truth Trust, 1993), 3–4.

7. Justification is God's astonishing declaration that all who are in Christ are righteous, based on two things: (1) the forgiveness of sin by Jesus' blood and (2) the imputation of Jesus' righteousness. For Jesus to accomplish our salvation, he had to meet the twofold demand of God's law (1) by perfectly obeying the law's demands of righteousness, (2) *so that* he could then perfectly pay the just penalty for our sin by coming under the full curse and condemnation of the law we deserve. The Bible teaches that all human beings are born "in Adam" (1 Cor. 15:22) and are under God's just curse of condemnation. Jesus came to regain for us what we lost in Adam by becoming the "last Adam" for us (v. 45), perfectly obeying God in the face of all the temptations that caused the first Adam to fail. Because of the last Adam's perfect righteousness for us, he alone could make the perfect sacrifice of his shed blood for us.

just demands by substituting his own Son on the cross for us. John Stott writes:

> The biblical meaning of the cross must always have at its center this principle of divine self-satisfaction through divine self-substitution. The biblical gospel of atonement is of God satisfying himself by substituting himself for us.[8]

Therefore, forgiving the sins of all who have faith in Jesus is now a perfectly just thing for God to do because he fully satisfied all the demands of his holy justice through the sinless life and sacrificial death of Jesus Christ in our place.[9]

OUR PRAYER for God's Forgiveness of Our Debts

God does not forgive our sins merely because we ask him for forgiveness by praying, "Forgive us our debts" (Matt. 6:12). Instead, the Bible teaches that the forgiveness of sins comes only through *repentance and faith* in Christ.[10] The prayer

---

8. John Stott, *The Cross of Christ* (InterVarsity Press, 1986), 158–59.

9. Paul teaches that the purpose of Jesus' death was not merely to redeem us by his blood (propitiation) to forgive our sins, but also *to demonstrate God's justice* by requiring nothing less than Jesus' blood to satisfy it. This was *"to show his righteousness* at the present time, so that he might be just and the justifier of the one who has faith in Jesus" (Rom. 3:26). Although God is always just, he didn't always look just during the Old Testament eras because he allowed people not to receive the penalty they deserved from him for their many sins. Paul tells us that this is not a demonstration of *God's injustice*, but a demonstration of *God's forbearance* because in God's "divine forbearance he had passed over former sins" (v. 25).

10. The resurrected Jesus told the apostles that *"repentance for the forgiveness of sins* should be proclaimed in his name to all nations" (Luke 24:47). We see Peter's obedience to this command in his preaching: *"Repent* therefore, and turn back, that your sins may be blotted out" (Acts 3:19). "To him all the prophets bear witness that everyone who *believes in him* receives forgiveness of sins through his name" (10:43).

through which we ask our Father in heaven to "forgive us our debts" expresses our repentance and faith in Christ.[11]

The Bible also uses words like "confess" to describe aspects of repentance and faith—such as when the apostle John writes: "If we *confess* our sins, he is faithful and just to forgive us our sins and to cleanse us from all unrighteousness" (1 John 1:9).[12] When we ask our heavenly Father to "forgive us our debts," we are repenting, believing, and confessing our sins.

If our heavenly Father completely forgives our sins when we repent and believe in Jesus Christ, why does Jesus teach us to keep asking our Father to forgive us our sins?

The Bible teaches that our justification is a one-time event that occurs when we first repent and believe, and it lasts forever. We will never be more justified, even when we're in heaven, than we are now.[13] So when we keep asking God to forgive our sins, we're not phasing in and out of God's love and forgiveness in between our times of repentance and faith.

The apostle John teaches that all justified believers continue to sin. He warns: "If we say we have no sin, we deceive ourselves, and the truth is not in us" (1 John 1:8). But he also teaches that God *continues cleansing believers from all their sins* by the blood of Jesus as they continue confessing their sins:

---

11. Repentance and faith are presented in Scripture as two sides of the same coin. Through repentance, we turn away from our sin, and through faith we turn to Christ as our Savior. When the Bible mentions only repentance, faith is assumed—such as when Paul proclaims: "Now he [God] commands all people everywhere to *repent*" (Acts 17:30). And when the Bible mentions only faith, repentance is assumed—such as when Paul declares: "Believe [have faith] in the Lord Jesus, and you will be saved" (16:31).

12. Paul writes: "If you *confess* with your mouth that Jesus is Lord and believe in your heart that God raised him from the dead, you will be saved" (Rom. 10:9).

13. Paul teaches that since we are "in Christ," God's love for us cannot be broken, because it's the same unbreakable love that the Father has for his only Son (Rom. 8:31–39).

If we walk in the light, as he is in the light, we have fellowship with one another, and the blood of Jesus his Son cleanses us from all sin. . . . If we confess our sins, he is faithful and just to forgive us our sins and to cleanse us from all unrighteousness. (1 John 1:7, 9)

God does not keep cleansing us (forgiving us) from our sin *because* we keep confessing our sin. Inevitably, all believers will die with some measure of unconfessed sin.[14] Our ongoing confession, repentance, and faith are not "good works" that we keep offering to God so that he will keep forgiving us.[15]

So why should believers who are justified continue to confess their sins?

Although our sins do not result in the loss of our heavenly Father's love and forgiveness, the Scriptures teach that our sins displease and grieve God and quench the transforming work of God's Spirit in our lives, shaping us into the image of Jesus.[16]

---

14. Some Christians are troubled when they think about failing to confess *all* their sins, especially before their death. Certainly, we should confess all our *known* sins. But it's not possible to know the depth of sin in our hearts. Jesus teaches: "For from within, out of the heart of man, come evil thoughts, sexual immorality, theft, murder, adultery, coveting, wickedness, deceit, sensuality, envy, slander, pride, foolishness. All these evil things come from within, and they defile a person" (Mark 7:21–23). The apostle John teaches that God does more than forgive the sins we *know and confess*. God is also faithful and just "to cleanse us from *all* unrighteousness" (1 John 1:9).

15. Instead, we keep confessing our sin *because* God promises to keep cleansing us from our sin through the blood of Jesus Christ. We are justified by faith alone, but the faith that justifies is not alone—it always shows itself in our ongoing confession, repentance, and faith. Our justification does not depend on our confession of sin, but those who are justified confess their sins.

16. "Do not *grieve* the Holy Spirit of God, by whom you were sealed for the day of redemption" (Eph. 4:30). "Do not *quench* the Spirit" (1 Thess. 5:19). "Do not neglect to do good and to share what you have, for such sacrifices are *pleasing* to God" (Heb. 13:16). "And without faith it is impossible to *please* him" (11:6). Because we are God's children, he promises to use all our sinful failures and trials not for our punishment but for our good, to help us grow and mature to be like his Son. Hebrews 12:10 tells us: "For they [our earthly fathers] disci-

But through our confession of sin, God promises to pour out
his mercy and grace to restore our broken fellowship with him
and help us in our time of need (Heb. 4:6, 16).

Paul tells us that God forgave King David, whom he considered to be his righteous (justified) son (Rom. 4:6–8). But David's
sin corrupted his soul, broke his transforming fellowship with
God, and robbed him of the joy of his salvation. Through
David's confession of sin, his relationship with God was
restored. God graciously recorded his confession for us:

> Purge me with hyssop, and I shall be clean; wash me, and I
> shall be whiter than snow. Let me hear joy and gladness; let
> the bones that you have broken rejoice. Hide your face from
> my sins, and blot out all my iniquities. Create in me a clean
> heart, O God, and renew a right spirit within me. Cast me not
> away from your presence, and take not your Holy Spirit from
> me. Restore to me the joy of your salvation, and uphold me
> with a willing spirit. (Ps. 51:7–12)[17]

---

plined us for a short time as it seemed best to them, but he [our heavenly
Father] disciplines us for good, that we may share in his holiness."

17. David's prayer, "Cast me not away from your presence, and take not your
Holy Spirit from me" (Ps. 51:11), reflects the enormous depth of his anxiety and
despair over his horrendous sins of adultery and murder (2 Samuel 12). David
was fearful that God would condemn him and remove the grace of his Holy
Spirit from him. He knows that if God judged him rightly for his sins, his
deserved end can only be destruction under the just outpouring of God's wrath.
So David begs the Lord for two things: (1) to forgive his sins (Ps. 51:1–6) and (2) to
restore his corrupt soul (vv. 7–12). There is significant discontinuity between
how God forgave Old Testament believers and indwelled them by his Holy
Spirit and how God does this with believers in Christ. But the Scriptures teach
that significant continuity is also found in God's unfolding covenant of grace
revealed in both old and new covenants. The Bible reveals a consistency
throughout, regarding how our unchanging God forgives and transforms his
people in all ages. Therefore, it is reasonable to affirm that David's experience
and prayer do not teach us that God will condemn and remove his Holy Spirit
from his people because of their sins. David's prayer should be seen as a
genuine expression of his realization that God does not owe him forgiveness
and restoration. David knew that God would be perfectly just to condemn him

When the apostle John tells us that God promises to "forgive us our sins" when we confess them (1 John 1:9), he is not using the word *forgive* in a legal sense. It's more like the forgiveness of a father for his dearly loved child when his child has done something wrong.

To help strengthen our experience of God's love and forgiveness when we sin, John reminds us of the ongoing intercessory work of Jesus for us as our *Advocate*: "My little children, I am writing these things to you so that you may not sin. But if anyone does sin, we have an *advocate* with the Father, Jesus Christ the righteous" (1 John 2:1).

Jesus' death and resurrection was not the end of his saving work for us. He ascended back to the right hand of God the Father to be our living, exalted High Priest who is always interceding for us before the Father's throne of grace. "Consequently, he is able to save to the uttermost those who draw near to God through him, since he always lives to make intercession for them" (Heb. 7:25).[18]

This doesn't mean that Jesus is trying to convince our heavenly Father to be merciful and not punish us for our sins, like a lawyer trying to convince a judge of the innocence of a client. It's not as if Jesus is for us but our Father is against us.

Instead, as strange as it may sound, Jesus' "case" on our behalf is an argument for us to receive God's justice. When we ask our Father to forgive our sins, God would be unjust to deny our request because he already condemned Jesus for our sin

---

for his sin and take his Holy Spirit from him, so David pleaded with God not to give him what he deserved, but to show him grace. God did that for David, and he promises to do that for all his people through Christ by grace. From first to last, the Christian life is a matter of grace. God's grace initiates our salvation, sustains our salvation, and will complete our salvation.

18. Paul asks: "Who is to condemn? Christ Jesus is the one who died—more than that, who was raised—who is at the right hand of God, who indeed is interceding for us" (Rom. 8:34).

and promised to accept us as righteous (justified) in his sight based on Jesus' perfect righteousness.[19]

When we pray and ask our Father to forgive us, we're not alone. Instead, we're joining our prayers with the prayers of Jesus as our High Priest before God's throne to receive God's mercy and find grace to help us.

> Since then we have a great high priest who has passed through the heavens, Jesus, the Son of God, . . . let us then with confidence draw near to the throne of grace, that we may receive mercy and find grace to help in time of need. (Heb. 4:14, 16)

Paul states: "Therefore, as you received Christ Jesus the Lord, so walk in him" (Col. 2:6).[20] We receive Christ through repentance and faith in him, and we continue walking in Christ the same way—through our ongoing repentance and faith in

---

19. God has made a covenant promise to always forgive us and cleanse us through Jesus' blood. Therefore, when we confess our sins, God demonstrates not merely his mercy but also his faithfulness and justice. God would not be just if he punished a believer in Christ. That would be like *double jeopardy* in a court of law. God *cannot* punish those who are in Christ because he already punished Jesus for their sins. As a believer, you can do nothing to cause God to love you any more, and you can do nothing to cause God to love you any less. The love he has for you is the same love he has for his one and only Son. You can please him by your faithfulness, and you can displease him by your sin. But he will never, and can never, reject you or disown you as his own. This is amazing grace.

20. Our experience of God's love and the forgiveness of our sins through faith in Christ has a past, present, and future tense: (1) We have been forgiven through Jesus' blood and righteousness when we first believed. This is our justification—a one-time event in the past—through which *we have been saved from sin's penalty.* (2) We are being forgiven through Jesus' blood and righteousness as we continue believing. This is our sanctification—an ongoing experience in the present—through which *we are being saved from sin's power.* (3) We will be forgiven through Jesus' blood and righteousness at the judgment day and forever in the new earth. This is our glorification in the future— through which *we will be saved from sin's presence.*

him as we continue asking our heavenly Father to forgive us our debts.[21]

CONCLUSION

When we ask our heavenly Father to "forgive us our debts," Jesus instructs us to include in our prayer the statement "*as we also have forgiven our debtors*" (Matt. 6:12). In Luke's record he writes, "Forgive us our sins, *for we ourselves forgive everyone who is indebted to us*" (Luke 11:4).

Jesus teaches that it is *necessary* for us to forgive others to receive the forgiveness of our heavenly Father. Immediately after his teaching on the Lord's Prayer, Jesus says, "*If you forgive others their trespasses*, your heavenly Father will also forgive you, but *if you do not forgive others their trespasses*, neither will your Father forgive your trespasses" (Matt. 6:14–15).[22]

But our forgiveness of others is not the *cause* of our forgive-

---

21. Here's a helpful example of a prayer of confession: "Most merciful God, we confess that we have sinned against you in thought, word, and deed, by what we have done, and by what we have left undone. We have not loved you with our whole heart; we have not loved our neighbors as ourselves. We are truly sorry and we humbly repent. For the sake of your Son Jesus Christ, have mercy on us and forgive us; that we may delight in your will, and walk in your ways, to the glory of your Name. Amen." *The Book of Common Prayer, and Administration of the Sacraments and Other Rites and Ceremonies of the Church, Together with the Psalter or Psalms of David, According to the Use of the Episcopal Church* (Church Publishing Incorporated, 1979), 360.

22. In Jesus' parable of the unforgiving servant, a man could not repay an enormous debt he owed a king, so he pleaded for mercy and the king graciously forgave him all his debt. But later, the man did not forgive a much smaller debt to someone who owed him. This enraged his master, who summoned the servant and said to him: "'You wicked servant! I forgave you all that debt because you pleaded with me. And should not you have had mercy on your fellow servant, as I had mercy on you?' And in anger his master delivered him to the jailers, until he should pay all his debt. So also my heavenly Father will do to every one of you, if you do not forgive your brother from your heart" (Matt. 18:32–35). James, the brother of Jesus, claims: "For judgment is without mercy to one who has shown no mercy" (James 2:13).

ness; it's the *evidence* that we are forgiven. Similarly, we're not justified by our good works. We're justified by faith alone, but the faith that justifies is revealed in our good works. Also, we're not forgiven by confessing our sins. We're forgiven by Christ alone. But those who are forgiven reveal it through confessing their sins.

Likewise, God does not forgive us because we forgive others. God forgives us because Jesus died for us. But we reveal our forgiveness by forgiving others.[23] Therefore, we should not ask God to forgive us unless we're willing to forgive those who sin against us.[24]

Forgiveness is not forgetting. It doesn't rationalize or minimize injustice and sin. It means that we imitate Christ by taking on ourselves the painful debts of the people who sinned against us by releasing them from the just penalty they deserve for their sin against us. When we forgive those who sin against us, we follow Jesus, who paid our debt that he did not owe because we owed a debt that we could not pay.

Augustine called this the *terrible petition* in the Lord's Prayer. But it's also a liberating one that includes not merely our liberation from sin by being forgiven but also our liberation from our bondage and bitterness toward those who sin against us.

"Forgive our sins as we forgive,"

---

23. J. I. Packer writes: "Those who live by God's forgiveness must imitate it; one whose only hope is that God will not hold his faults against him forfeits his right to hold others' faults against them. Do as you would be done by is the rule here, and the unforgiving Christian brands himself a hypocrite." J. I. Packer, *Growing in Christ* (Crossway, 1977), 193. Leon Morris explains: "We have no right to seek forgiveness for our own sins if we are withholding forgiveness from others." Leon Morris, *The Gospel According to Matthew* (Eerdmans, 1992), 147.

24. Robert Louis Stevenson, the author of *Treasure Island*, used to pray the Lord's Prayer with his family every day. One day, in the middle of this prayer, he got up from his knees and left the room. His wife ran after him, thinking that he was ill. "What's the matter?" she asked. "Are you ill?" "No," he answered, "but I am not fit to pray the Lord's Prayer today."

you taught us, Lord, to pray;
but you alone can grant us grace
to live the words we say.

How can your pardon reach and bless
   the unforgiving heart
   that broods on wrongs, and will not let
   old bitterness depart?

In blazing light your Cross reveals
   the truth we dimly knew,
   how small the debts men owe to us,
   how great our debt to you.

Lord, cleanse the depths within our souls,
   and bid resentment cease;
   then, reconciled to God and man,
   our lives will spread your peace.[25]

Step Six: Answer the Review Questions with Answer Key

Try to answer the Review Questions below on your own before you refer to the Answer Key in the back of the book.

1. What is the debt that you owe to God?[i]
2. How does God forgive your debts?[ii]
3. Why should believers who are justified continue to confess their sins?[iii]
4. Why does Jesus teach you to forgive others in your prayers for forgiveness?[iv]

---

25. Rosamond E. Herklots, "Forgive Our Sins as We Forgive" (1969).

Step Seven: Answer the Discussion Questions with Sample Answers

Reflect on these questions either individually or in a group. They are intended to renew your understanding, stir your heart's desires, and deepen your love for God and others. Try to answer each question on your own before consulting the sample answers in the Answer Key.

1. Mind for Truth: Why is forgiveness not necessarily forgetting the sins of those who have sinned against you?[v]
2. Heart for God: How does your continual repentance and faith set your heart affections more on God daily?[vi]
3. Life for Ministry: How does God's forgiveness of your sin change the way you treat those who wrong you?[vii]

Step Eight: Take the Review Quiz with Answer Key

This quiz is designed to help you recall and apply key concepts you're learning, increasing your understanding of these concepts for practical application in life and ministry. Try to answer each question on your own before you refer to the Answer Key.

1. In what ways are we failing to fulfill our obligations to God? (Choose all that apply.)
   a. when we commit sins of commission
   b. when we commit sins of omission
   c. when we fail to forgive others who have wronged us
   d. when we fail to pray the prayer of forgiveness

e. when we fail to pray for our forgiveness

2. What is the great dilemma presented to us in Scripture?
   a. how man can be restored to God in his relationship
   b. how a holy and just God can forgive our sins without being unjust
   c. how the New Testament fulfills the Old Testament
   d. how Jesus Christ became man

3. "God does not forgive our sins merely because we ask him for forgiveness by praying, 'Forgive us our debts.'"
   a. true
   b. false

4. Why does Jesus teach us to keep asking our Father to forgive us our sins even when we repent and believe in Jesus Christ?
   a. because we keep phasing in and out of God's love and forgiveness
   b. because we should not die with some measure of unconfessed sin
   c. because those who are forgiven show it by drawing near to God in repentance and faith
   d. because we need to keep up our "good works" so that he will keep forgiving us

5. Forgiveness of others is not the _____, but the _____ of our forgiveness.
   a. cause; evidence
   b. evidence; cause
   c. fruit; root

d. claim; profession

6. When you forgive someone, you _____. (Choose all that apply.)
  a. rationalize and minimize the person's sins
  b. reveal that you have been forgiven
  c. follow Jesus, who paid your debt that you could not pay
  d. phase into God's love and forgiveness

Answer Key

Chapter 5 quiz answers are found in the Answer Key.[viii]

Step Nine: Meditate and Pray

All theology should lead us to doxology. The ultimate goal of learning biblical and theological truths is not just to renew our minds, but also to renew our heart affections so that our lives are renewed to the honor of God. Pause now to meditate on and pray about what God is teaching you in his Word. After you pray, consider recording any new insights for application later. Use this prayer outline below if you find it helpful.

- Praise God for providing for you in Jesus Christ what he justly demands of you in his law.
- Confess your rebellion of withholding your forgiveness from those who wrong you.
- Thank the Lord Jesus for interceding as your High Priest so that you can receive God's mercy and find grace to help you.
- Ask the Holy Spirit to give you strength to take on the painful debt of those who sin against you by releasing them from the just penalty they deserve.

Here is an example of how you can pray through the petition "Forgive us our debts, as we also have forgiven our debtors" in the Lord's Prayer. You can use this as a guide during personal devotions, with your family, in small groups, or with your congregation.

> *Our Father in heaven, we humbly acknowledge that we owe you a debt that we can never repay because of our many sins. Yet through the perfect life, sacrificial death, and resurrection of Jesus Christ in our place, you have made a way for our immense debt to be forgiven. Cleanse us from all our sins and help us to live in the freedom and joy of knowing that we are fully forgiven and justified in your sight through Jesus' blood and righteousness. As you have forgiven us for our sins, grant us the grace to forgive those who have wronged us. Just as you have mercifully released us from our debts, give us the power to release others from what they owe us. Free our hearts from resentment and bitterness. Teach us to reflect your mercy by forgiving as we have been forgiven. May your forgiveness bring reconciliation and peace, allowing us to reflect to others the abundant that mercy we have received from you.*

Step Ten: Go Deeper as a Lifelong Learner

This step encourages your deeper exploration by using key resources drawn from the chapter article and academic notes to help you grow in your understanding and application of biblical truths, promoting your lifelong learning and continued growth in spiritual maturity.

BIBLE PASSAGES

Gain a deeper understanding and application of the key biblical passages from the chapter article through more in-depth reading, reflection, study, memorization, and meditation.

> "The LORD passed before him and proclaimed, 'The LORD, the LORD, a God merciful and gracious, slow to anger, and abounding in steadfast love and faithfulness, keeping steadfast love for thousands, forgiving iniquity and transgression and sin, but who will by no means clear the guilty, visiting the iniquity of the fathers on the children and the children's children, to the third and the fourth generation.'" (Exod. 34:6–7)

> "Purge me with hyssop, and I shall be clean; wash me, and I shall be whiter than snow. Let me hear joy and gladness; let the bones that you have broken rejoice. Hide your face from my sins, and blot out all my iniquities. Create in me a clean heart, O God, and renew a right spirit within me. Cast me not away from your presence, and take not your Holy Spirit from me. Restore to me the joy of your salvation, and uphold me with a willing spirit." (Ps. 51:7–12)

> "You therefore must be perfect, as your heavenly Father is perfect." (Matt. 5:48)

> "But when the Pharisees heard that he had silenced the Sadducees, they gathered together. And one of them, a lawyer, asked him a question to test him. 'Teacher, which is the great commandment in the Law?' And he said to him, 'You shall love the Lord your God with all your heart and with all your soul and with all your mind. This is the great and first commandment. And a second is like it: You shall

love your neighbor as yourself. On these two commandments depend all the Law and the Prophets.'" (Matt. 22:34–
40)

"But now the righteousness of God has been manifested apart
from the law, although the Law and the Prophets bear witness
to it—the righteousness of God through faith in Jesus Christ
for all who believe. For there is no distinction: for all have
sinned and fall short of the glory of God, and are justified by
his grace as a gift, through the redemption that is in Christ
Jesus, whom God put forward as a propitiation by his blood, to
be received by faith. This was to show God's righteousness,
because in his divine forbearance he had passed over former
sins." (Rom. 3:21–25)

"David also speaks of the blessing of the one to whom God
counts righteousness apart from works: 'Blessed are those
whose lawless deeds are forgiven, and whose sins are covered;
blessed is the man against whom the Lord will not count his
sin.'" (Rom. 4:6–8)

"For our sake he made him to be sin who knew no sin, so that
in him we might become the righteousness of God." (2 Cor.
5:21)

"Yet we know that a person is not justified by works of the law
but through faith in Jesus Christ, so we also have believed in
Christ Jesus, in order to be justified by faith in Christ and not
by works of the law, because by works of the law no one will
be justified." (Gal. 2:16)

"Since then we have a great high priest who has passed
through the heavens, Jesus, the Son of God, let us hold fast our
confession. . . . Let us then with confidence draw near to the

throne of grace, that we may receive mercy and find grace to help in time of need." (Heb. 4:14, 16)

"Consequently, he is able to save to the uttermost those who draw near to God through him, since he always lives to make intercession for them." (Heb. 7:25)

"For whoever keeps the whole law but fails in one point has become guilty of all of it." (James 2:10)

"It is written, 'You shall be holy, for I am holy.' And if you call on him as Father who judges impartially according to each one's deeds, conduct yourselves with fear throughout the time of your exile." (1 Peter 1:16–17)

"But if we walk in the light, as he is in the light, we have fellowship with one another, and the blood of Jesus his Son cleanses us from all sin. . . . If we confess our sins, he is faithful and just to forgive us our sins and to cleanse us from all unrighteousness." (1 John 1:7, 9)

"My little children, I am writing these things to you so that you may not sin. But if anyone does sin, we have an advocate with the Father, Jesus Christ the righteous." (1 John 2:1)

"Therefore, as you received Christ Jesus the Lord, so walk in him." (Col. 2:6)

CATECHISMS

Explore key biblical truths through historic Christian catechisms that offer clear guidance on their meaning and life application.

Westminster Shorter Catechism (Q. 105)

- Q. 105: What do we pray for in the fifth petition?
- A. In the fifth petition, which is, And forgive us our debts, as we forgive our debtors, we pray that God, for Christ's sake, would freely pardon all our sins; which we are the rather encouraged to ask, because by his grace we are enabled from the heart to forgive others.

Westminster Larger Catechism (Q. 194)

- Q. 194: What do we pray for in the fifth petition?
- A. In the fifth petition (which is, *Forgive us our debts, as we forgive our debtors*), acknowledging that we and all others are guilty both of original and actual sin, and thereby become debtors to the justice of God; and that neither we, nor any other creature, can make the least satisfaction for that debt: we pray for ourselves and others, that God of his free grace would, through the obedience and satisfaction of Christ, apprehended and applied by faith, acquit us both from the guilt and punishment of sin, accept us in his Beloved; continue his favor and grace to us, pardon our daily failings, and fill us with peace and joy, in giving us daily more and more assurance of forgiveness; which we are the rather emboldened to ask, and encouraged to expect, when we have this testimony in ourselves, that we from the heart forgive others their offenses.

Heidelberg Catechism (Q. 126)

- Q. 126: What does the fifth petition mean?

- A. "Forgive us our debts, as we also have forgiven our debtors" means: Because of Christ's blood, do not hold against us, poor sinners that we are, any of the sins we do or the evil that constantly clings to us. Forgive us just as we are fully determined, as evidence of your grace in us, to forgive our neighbors.

BOOKS

Expand your understanding of key biblical concepts through selected books that offer more in-depth exploration and practical application.

- John Murray, *Redemption Accomplished and Applied*— Murray provides a thorough analysis of the atonement, explaining how Christ's death secures forgiveness and redemption, covering both the accomplishment of salvation and its personal application.

- John Stott, *The Cross of Christ*—Stott's classic work on the atonement dives into the meaning of Christ's sacrifice, examining how his death brings about forgiveness of sins. This book is a thorough exploration of the cross and the forgiveness it offers to humanity.

- Timothy Keller, *The Prodigal God: Recovering the Heart of the Christian Faith*—Keller uses the parable of the prodigal son to reveal God's lavish grace and forgiveness, calling both rebels and the self-righteous to experience God's transforming forgiveness and love.

HYMNS

Allow these biblical truths to lead you to praise and worship God with prayers and hymns that honor God for who he is and what he does.

- "O Sacred Head, Now Wounded," by Bernard of Clairvaux—This hymn focuses on the depth of Christ's sacrificial suffering for believers, inviting them to reflect on his sacrifice and respond with humility, gratitude, and devotion for his astonishing love.

- "Amazing Grace," by John Newton—This beloved hymn exalts God's amazing grace and mercy that rescues and transforms sinners. It invites believers to rejoice in his forgiveness and respond with heartfelt gratitude and devotion.

- "When I Survey the Wondrous Cross," by Isaac Watts—This classic hymn invites believers to reflect on Christ's ultimate sacrifice on the cross for them and respond with awe, a heart of gratitude, and a life of devotion for God's boundless love.

6

OUR PROTECTION

Step One: Read the Introduction

L ife is a battle that involves dangerous spiritual warfare that we cannot overcome by ourselves, so Jesus instructs us to ask our heavenly Father for protection by praying, "Our Father[,] . . . lead us not into temptation, but deliver us from evil" (Matt. 6:9, 13).

The Bible is filled with examples of God's purposefully leading his people into times of temptation and testing. God never tempts us in the sense of enticing us to sin; instead, he brings trials into our lives to transform us into the image of his Son. We should not be surprised by trials but learn to accept them as necessary for our growth.

Why should we ask God to spare us these temptations if they are necessary for our growth and flourishing? We ask our Father *not* to lead us into temptation because we know how vulnerable we are and how easy it is for us to fail God's tests. When it is our Father's will to lead us into temptation, we join with Jesus, in reliance on the power of his Holy Spirit, and cry out to our Father for his grace and mercy to endure the temptation as we pray, "Not as I will, but as you will" (Matt. 26:39).

Jesus instructs us to plead with our heavenly Father to "deliver us from evil," or we will almost certainly fail the test. Satan terrorizes with evil outwardly through the world and inwardly through our flesh. Although our deliverance from evil must be the work of God's Holy Spirit, the Bible teaches that we're always to be active in this process, trusting his promises never to tempt us beyond our ability and always to provide for us a way of escape.

In this chapter, you will learn to request God not to lead us into temptation but deliver us from evil.

Step Two: Review the Learning Goals

Learning Goals

In this chapter, you will be equipped to:

- Pray that God will use temptations to transform us into Christ's image.
- Pray that our temptations would not lead us to disobey God, and for grace to rely on God's Spirit when temptations come.
- Pray for deliverance from outward and inward attacks of Satan.
- Pray that our temptations would deepen our trust in the Father and draw us to him.

Step Three: Review the Key Ideas

Key Ideas

In this chapter, these are the key ideas:

- God will not entice us to be subdued by the power and control of temptation but will lead us into temptations to transform us into the image of his Son.
- We are vulnerable to failing God's tests because of our sinful nature, but we learn to rely on God's Spirit as we endure temptations that are God's will.
- Satan entices us to sin outwardly by the world and inwardly by our sinful nature.
- We learn to trust God's promises by drawing near to him while enduring temptations.

Step Four: Answer the Reflection Questions

Take a moment before reading the chapter article to reflect on these questions. They'll help you connect your beliefs, desires, and practices with the topics ahead, allowing for deeper engagement and more practical application to your life and ministry.

1. Do you think that God purposefully leads us into temptation?
2. How do you think God helps us when we are tempted to sin?

Step Five: Read the Chapter Article with Academic Notes

After Jesus instructs us to ask our heavenly Father for our daily physical needs and for the forgiveness of our sins, he instructs us to pray for our third basic need in life—our protection. "Pray then like this: 'Our Father[,] . . . lead us not into temptation, but deliver us from evil'" (Matt. 6:9, 13).[1]

---

1.   This is one petition that consists of two parts. These two clauses are linked

This last petition expresses one primary concept: life is a battle that involves dangerous spiritual warfare that we cannot overcome by ourselves, so we must trust our heavenly Father to protect us.

What does it mean to ask our heavenly Father not to lead us into temptation? Will God purposefully lead us into situations that will tempt us to sin? That God would lead us into temptation has confused and troubled many followers of Jesus throughout history.[2]

In this verse, the Greek word translated "temptation" (πειρασμόν) conveys the idea of an experiment, a trial, or a test that proves or gives evidence of something. The words *temptation, trial,* and *test* are used synonymously in the Bible for hardships we experience that help our faith mature (James 1:2–4).

In all forms of good education, teachers give students *tests* that are designed to help the students learn and give evidence of their progress. Students don't normally like taking tests, but they usually understand why tests are necessary.

Similarly, the Scriptures teach that God gives us tests, also translated "trials," to help us flourish in our relationship with him and in our fulfillment of his kingdom purposes for our lives. Like most students, however, we don't enjoy taking God's tests because they are often painful.

God Leads Us into Temptation

So does God lead us into temptation? The biblical answer depends on the meaning of the word *temptation*. The problem

---

by the Greek conjunction ἀλλά. The first clause, "Lead us not into temptation," is amplified and applied by the second clause, *"but* [ἀλλά] deliver us from evil." Luke's record of the Lord's Prayer does not include the second clause (Luke 11:4).

2. If this petition means only "Do not allow us to enter into temptation" or "Do not let us yield to temptation," why did Jesus instruct us to ask our heavenly Father not to *lead us* into temptation?

is that the same Greek word used for "temptation" (πειρασμόν) in the New Testament can have different meanings.

The Bible contains numerous examples of God's purposefully leading his people into times of temptation and testing.[3] So in this sense, our Father allows us to be "tempted" in that he allows us to be "tested" by leading us into difficult circumstances to help us grow. This is how Jesus uses the word *temptation* when he teaches the Lord's Prayer.

James uses the same Greek word for "temptation" that Jesus uses, but with a different meaning.[4] James writes, "Let no one say when he is tempted, 'I am being tempted by God,' for God cannot be tempted with evil, and he himself tempts no one" (James 1:13).[5] So when God brings "times of testing" into our

---

3. Soon after God created Adam and Eve and placed them in the garden paradise, he tested them (Genesis 3). In Genesis 22:1 we read that "God tested Abraham." After God delivered the first generation of Israelites from bondage in Egypt, he tested them in the wilderness (Numbers 14; Psalm 95). The same Greek word translated "temptation" (πειρασμόν) in Matthew 6:13 is also used in the Greek translation of the Hebrew Old Testament (Septuagint) in passages such as Numbers 14 and Psalm 95. God called Israel to be fruitful and multiply (Gen. 1:27–28; 35:11) and to obey all his commands in order to have life (Lev. 18:5). But like Adam, Israel failed God's tests. God's commands for Israel to make sacrifices for sin were reminders of his people's failure of his tests to keep his demands and their need to look ahead for God's promised Redeemer.

4. Similarly, the New Testament uses the same Greek word for "justification" (δικαιοῦται), but its meaning varies based on the context in which it is found. It means "declared righteousness," but our works are proof, according to James, that our faith is genuine, that it is a true, living faith. James's point is that we are justified not by a dead faith, but by a faith that works. God "declares" us righteous on the basis of that faith that works. The works do "prove" our faith, but the way they do this is by showing that our faith is real. So justification is by faith and *not* by works, but works serve as evidence that the faith is authentic. Paul clarifies: "We know that a person is not justified [δικαιοῦται] by works of the law but through faith in Jesus Christ" (Gal. 2:16). James adds: "You see that a person is justified [δικαιοῦται] by works and not by faith alone" (James 2:24).

5. James tells us that "God *cannot* be tempted with evil." God's nature is "untemptable" (ἀπείραστός). Just as the Scriptures teach that God is not capable of changing, lying, or breaking a promise, God is not capable of being tempted or seduced by things that are evil. Therefore, God is not capable of tempting (evil luring) anyone to sin.

lives, he never tempts us in the sense of "enticing" or "luring" us to sin.

God leads us into places in which we will experience temptation. But God never leads us into the power and control of temptation to be subdued by it.[6] James teaches that the origin of that kind of lure and enticement to temptation is not from God, but from our own sinful hearts: "Each person is tempted when he is *lured and enticed by his own desire*" (James 1:14).[7]

Luke uses this same word to describe Jesus' experience during his forty days in the wilderness before his public ministry: "When the devil had ended every *temptation* [πειρασμὸν], he departed from him until an opportune time" (Luke 4:12–13).[8] In Hebrews 4:15, Jesus is described as "one who in every respect *has been tempted* as we are, yet without sin."[9]

Therefore, just as God led Adam, Abraham, Israel, and Jesus into temptations for their good and his glory, God also leads us into temptations. Paul sees these times of temptation and suffering as essential, continuing, normal experiences for all true followers of Jesus.[10] Peter says: "Beloved, do not be

---

6. In his *Confessions*, Augustine helps us distinguish between the two different meanings of the same word for "temptation" when he writes, "All men must *be tempted*; but to *be brought into temptation* is to be brought into the power and the control of temptation; it is to not only *be subjected* to temptation but to *be subdued* by temptation."

7. Our sinful human nature (flesh) by itself has the power to entice us to sin. But Satan often tempts us through our sinful human nature. We'll study how Satan tempts us through our "flesh" and the "world" later in this chapter.

8. Paul presents Jesus as the *second man* and the *last Adam* (1 Cor. 15:45–47). Adam, the *first man*, was tempted in the garden and failed to obey God, resulting in eternal death for humanity (Rom. 5:12–14). But when the *second man*, Jesus, was similarly tempted throughout his life, he perfectly obeyed God, resulting in eternal life for humanity (vv. 18–19).

9. The question arises, "If God cannot be tempted and Jesus is God, how can Jesus be tempted?" The Bible teaches that Jesus is a divine person with a divine nature and a human nature. Since Jesus is the divine, eternal Son of God, he cannot be tempted. In his humanity, however, Jesus experienced real human limitations and temptations (Heb. 2:17–18; 4:14–16).

10. When Paul reflects on his many temptations, he writes, "We are afflicted in

surprised at *the fiery trial when it comes upon you to test you*, as though something strange were happening to you" (1 Peter 4:12).

In our Father's great love for us, he brings trials into our lives. We should not be surprised by them but learn to accept them as a vital part of God's normal plan to transform us into the image of his Son.

Asking God *Not* to Lead Us into Temptation

Since God leads us into times of temptation for our good and his glory, then why does Jesus instruct us to ask our Father in heaven *not* to lead us into temptation? Why should we ask God to spare us these temptations if they are necessary for us to grow and flourish spiritually?

J. I. Packer writes: "Temptation may be our lot, but only a fool will make it his preference."[11] Peter and Paul did not ask God to lead them into temptation, and neither should we. Instead, they learned the opposite from Jesus—to ask God *not* to lead them into temptation.

In the garden of Gethsemane, when Jesus contemplated God's will for him to take the fullness of God's wrath on himself on the cross for our forgiveness, his first response was to cry out, "My Father, if it be possible, let this cup pass from me" (Matt. 26:39). In essence, Jesus was praying, "Father, if it is possible, do not lead me into this temptation."[12]

Jesus soon realized, however, that his Father's will was to lead him to the cross, even though he would be tempted to turn

---

every way, but not crushed; perplexed, but not driven to despair; persecuted, but not forsaken; struck down, but not destroyed; always carrying in the body the death of Jesus, so that the life of Jesus may also be manifested in our bodies" (2 Cor. 4:8–10).

11. J. I. Packer, *Growing in Christ* (Crossway, 1977), 196.

12. This is not a serene or stoic prayer, but a prayer made "in agony ... [as] his sweat became like great drops of blood falling down to the ground" (Luke 22:44).

away from his Father's plan. Only by resisting this temptation and enduring the cross could he remain faithful and secure salvation for his people.

Only by overcoming this temptation could Jesus come to know "the joy that was set before him" and become "the founder and perfecter of our faith" (Heb. 12:2). So he submitted to this trial and prayed, "Nevertheless, not as I will, but as you will" (Matt. 26:39).

While Jesus was experiencing his temptation in the garden, he reminded his disciples to pray that they will not enter temptation. "Watch and pray that you may not enter into temptation. The spirit indeed is willing, but the flesh is weak" (Matt. 26:41).[13]

His disciples were especially vulnerable to temptation because they were so tired that they kept falling asleep (Matt. 26:43). Jesus knew that although their "spirit" was willing to obey his instruction to watch and pray, the physical tiredness and weakness of their "flesh" (body) could lead them to disobey him.

We ask our Father *not* to lead us into temptation because we know how vulnerable we are and how easy it is for us to fail God's tests. And we know how horrible the consequences of our failure could be to ourselves, others, and God's name.[14]

When it is our Father's will to lead us into temptation, however, we join with Jesus in reliance on the power of his Holy

---

13. The Greek words that Jesus uses here are *spirit* (πνεῦμα) and *flesh* (σὰρξ). Jesus' statement "the flesh is weak" in this context is a reference to the weak physical bodies of his disciples. But Paul uses the same Greek word *flesh* (σὰρξ) to mean our "sinful desires" (see Rom. 7:18; 13:14; Gal. 5:13, 16–24). Although the Bible refers to our physical bodies as being weak and susceptible to evil influence, it does not characterize the physical body as evil in itself. The physical world and our bodies were created by God as good and will be re-created good when Jesus returns to make all things new.

14. Paul warns us: "Therefore let anyone who thinks that he stands take heed lest he fall" (1 Cor. 10:12).

Spirit and cry out to our Father for his grace and mercy to endure the temptation as we pray, "Not as I will, but as you will" (Matt. 26:39).[15]

ASKING God to Deliver Us from Evil

Jesus instructs us that when God leads us into temptation, we should plead with our heavenly Father to "deliver us from evil" (Matt. 6:13), or we will almost certainly fail the test.[16] The word translated "deliver" (ῥῦσαι) is a strong word that conveys the idea of our desperate need to be "rescued" from great danger when being tempted.[17]

The Greek word translated "evil" can refer to evil in general or to the "Evil One," Satan, in particular.[18] Jesus is most likely

---

15. When our Father leads us into temptation, we are thankful not for the temptation itself, but for how God will use it for our ultimate good and the fulfillment of his kingdom purposes through us. After James writes, *"Count it all joy . . . when you meet trials of various kinds"* (James 1:2), he then tells us the reason that we count it all joy: "for you know that the testing of your faith produces steadfastness. And let steadfastness have its full effect, that you may be perfect and complete, lacking in nothing" (vv. 3–4). Believers should grieve and mourn tragedies, terminal illnesses, and death. When Jesus' friend Lazarus died, Jesus was not joyful and thankful to God for his death. He saw death, like Satan, as his enemy that he hates and that he had come to conquer. So he wept when he learned that Lazarus had died. But Jesus gave thanks to his Father at the tomb of Lazarus for how he was going to use his death to display the Father's glory by raising him from the dead (John 11:38–44).

16. John Calvin explains: "We conclude from this petition, that we have no strength for living a holy life, except so far as we obtain it from God. Whoever implores the assistance of God to overcome temptations, acknowledges that, unless God deliver him, he will be constantly falling." John Calvin, *Commentary on the Gospel of Matthew*, trans. William Pringle (Edinburgh: Banner of Truth Trust, 1958).

17. At the crucifixion of Jesus, the religious leaders mocked him by saying, "He trusts in God; let God *deliver* [ῥῦσαι] him now" (Matt. 27:43). In Paul's struggle with the temptations of his sinful nature, he cries out to be rescued, using this same word: "Wretched man that I am! Who will *deliver* [ῥῦσαι] me from this body of death?" (Rom. 7:24).

18. There is debate among New Testament scholars regarding the meaning of

referring to both here. Three sources of evil are the enemy of our soul: the *world*, the *flesh*, and the *devil*.[19]

But our primary foe is the devil, Satan, who is the personification and instigator of all evil.[20] The Scriptures teach that Satan is a fallen angel who terrorizes the world through all kinds of evil. He causes great havoc throughout God's redemptive story, starting with Adam and continuing with Job, Abraham, Moses, David, Jesus, and the apostles.[21]

Satan uses two primary strategies of attack to entice us to sin: (1) an *outward attack* by use of the *world* and (2) an *inward attack* by use of our *flesh* (our sinful human nature).

Satan's *outward attack* is through the lure of a sinful *world*

τοῦ πονηροῦ. The use of the definite article (τοῦ) can refer to evil in general (neuter gender), the Evil One (masculine gender), or both.

19. The world, the flesh, and the devil are sometimes called the "Unholy Trinity." Paul refers to all three sources of evil in Ephesians 2:1–3: "And you were dead in the trespasses and sins in which you once walked, following the course of this *world*, following the *prince of the power of the air* [*devil*], the spirit that is now at work in the sons of disobedience—among whom we all once lived in the passions of our *flesh*." To invoke a threefold pattern found elsewhere in this book and series, Satan is "normative," the would-be ruler of this world; the world itself is "situational," the configuration of evil in historical events; and the flesh is "existential," within ourselves as our fallen nature. A similar pattern appears in the temptation of Eve in Genesis 3:6, when she accepts the serpent's view that the forbidden fruit brings wisdom (normative), is good for food (existential), and is pleasant to the eye (situational). But when Jesus was tempted, he rejected Satan's claims: he would not obey Satan to satisfy his hunger (existential), to display his power to the world (situational), or to engage in false worship (normative).

20. In the Old Testament, the Hebrew word for "Satan" (שָׂטָן) is a generic noun meaning "accuser" or "adversary." In the New Testament, the Greek word *devil* (διάβολος), meaning "slanderer," is used with *Satan* interchangeably as a synonym. Matthew calls Satan "the tempter" (Matt. 4:3). John calls him "the ruler of this world" (John 12:31; 14:30). Paul calls him "the prince of the power of the air" (Eph. 2:2) and "the god of this world" (2 Cor. 4:4). In Scripture, both good and evil are fundamentally personal, not abstractions or inanimate forces. God is personal goodness, Satan personal evil.

21. Matthew writes that when our Father, by the power of his Holy Spirit, led Jesus into temptation to prepare him for his public ministry, "Jesus was led up by the Spirit into the wilderness *to be tempted by the devil*" (Matt. 4:1).

with all its false promises of lasting satisfaction and joy. When Paul writes that "you once walked, following *the course of this world*" (Eph. 2:2), he's referring to ungodly societal beliefs, values, and behaviors that Satan uses to tempt followers of Jesus to disobey God.[22]

Satan's *inward attack* includes appealing to our sinful human nature with all its lusts, greed, and pride so that we look for true happiness and fulfillment other than God.

Jesus taught that all our external sins of the body come from the internal sins of our morally corrupt heart (Mark 7:20–23).[23]

Although our deliverance from evil must be the work of God's Holy Spirit, the Bible teaches that we're always to be active in this process.[24] Lying behind our every human exertion is the Holy Spirit's life-transforming power (Phil. 2:12–13).

So when we ask our heavenly Father to "deliver us from evil" in all its forms, we're putting on our spiritual armor (Eph.

---

22. Church historian Richard Lovelace explains that "when *world* is used in a negative sense in Scripture, what is meant is the total system of corporate flesh operating on earth under satanic control. . . . Included are dehumanizing social, economic and political systems; business operations and foreign policy based on local interest at the expense of general human welfare; and culturally pervasive institutionalized sin such as racism. . . . Much of the Christian community today is deeply penetrated by worldly patterns of thinking, motivation and behavior, and thus its spiritual life is deadened and its witness rendered ineffectual." Richard Lovelace, *Dynamics of Spiritual Life: An Evangelical Theology of Renewal* (IVP Academic, 1979), 93–94.

23. At its core, sin is more than disobeying God's laws. It is a deep-seated, invisible, terminal disease. Paul describes the actions of our sinful hearts as the works of the flesh (Gal. 5:19–21). He writes, "Those who belong to Christ Jesus have crucified *the flesh* with its *passions and desires*" (v. 24).

24. The Scriptures teach that we overcome temptation by learning how to turn away from sin *in repentance* and turn to Jesus Christ *in faith*. Paul presents repentance as putting off the old self and faith as putting on the new self (Romans 6; Colossians 3). In repentance, we pull our heart's affections away from idols that can never satisfy so that we can place our affections onto the ascended Jesus Christ, who alone can satisfy. Then we experience what the Puritans called "the expulsive power of a new affection."

6:10–18), humbling ourselves and resisting the devil (James 4:7), and drawing near to God (v. 8) for his grace and mercy to protect us so that we will remain "steadfast under trial" (1:12).

God graciously gives us two invaluable promises in Scripture to help us overcome temptation.

His first promise is that he will not tempt us beyond what we can handle. Paul says: "No temptation has overtaken you that is not common to man. God is faithful, and *he will not let you be tempted beyond your ability*" (1 Cor. 10:13).[25] And God's second promise is to provide us with everything we need to overcome temptation: "But with the temptation *he will also provide the way of escape, that you may be able to endure it*" (v. 13).

As we learn to endure temptation and draw near to God for help, we learn to trust in his promises never to tempt us beyond our ability and always to provide for us a way of escape.

CONCLUSION

James writes: "'God opposes the proud but gives grace to the humble.' Submit yourselves therefore to God. Resist the devil, and he will flee from you" (James 4:6–7).[26] Although

---

25. God graciously limits the specific temptations we experience so that they are within our ability to resist and overcome. Calvin writes, "God alleviates temptations, that they may not overpower us by their weight. For he knows the measure of our power, which he has himself conferred. According to that, *he regulates our temptations.*" John Calvin, *Commentary on the Sermon on the Mount*, trans. William Pringle (Banner of Truth Trust, 1959).

26. Paul exhorts: "Finally, be strong in the Lord and in the strength of his might. Put on the whole armor of God, that you may be able to stand against the schemes of the devil. For we do not wrestle against flesh and blood, but against the rulers, against the authorities, against the cosmic powers over this present darkness, against the spiritual forces of evil in the heavenly places. Therefore take up the whole armor of God, that you may be able to withstand in the evil day, and having done all, to stand firm" (Eph. 6:10–13).

Satan is fierce,[27] God promises that he will flee from us when we resist him and draw near to God.[28]

We should respect Satan, but not fear him. Satan and God are not equal opposites. Satan is a false god. He is a creature in rebellion against his Creator.

It's only in the fighting against temptations that God leads us to new levels of dependence on him and leads us to newer and deeper levels of joy, love, peace, and power. John Bunyan writes, "Temptation provokes me to look upward to God."[29]

Temptation itself is not sin. Temptation is the temptation *to sin*. Jesus was tempted (Matt. 4:1), but he never sinned (Heb. 4:15–16). Temptation becomes sin only when we give in to it.[30] Sin occurs when we fail to resist temptation and allow it to lead us to disobey God in our thoughts, words, or deeds.[31]

---

27. Peter warns: "Be sober-minded; be watchful. Your adversary the devil prowls around like a roaring lion, seeking someone to devour. Resist him, firm in your faith, knowing that the same kinds of suffering are being experienced by your brotherhood throughout the world" (1 Peter 5:8–9).

28. "God is strong enough to free you from everything and can do you more good than all the devils can do you harm. All that God decrees is that you confide in him, that you draw near him, that you trust him and distrust yourself, and so be helped; and with this help you will defeat whatever hell brings against you. Never lose hold of this firm hope even if the demons are legion and all kinds of severe temptations harass you. Lean upon Him, because if the Lord is not your support and your strength, then you will fall and you will be afraid of everything." John of Avila, *Sermons*, trans. Richard M. H. Smith (Catholic University of America Press, 1987), no.9, First Sunday of Lent.

29. John Bunyan, quoted in *The Treasury of Inspirational Anecdotes, Quotations, and Illustrations*, comp. E. Paul Hovey (Fleming H. Revell, 1994), 276.

30. John Owen, the Puritan theologian, writes: "Sin will not die unless it be constantly weakened. Spare it, and it will heal its wounds, and recover its strength. We must continually watch against the operations of this principle of (indwelling) sin . . . in all that we do! . . . Let no man think to kill sin with a few gentle strokes. He, who has once smitten the serpent, if he does not follow his blow until it is killed, may repent that he ever began the quarrel in the first place; and so will he who undertakes to deal with sin, if he does not pursue it constantly to death; sin will revive, and the man must die." John Owen, *On Mortification of Sin* (1656; repr., Banner of Truth Trust, 2004).

31. The Bible gives three practical directives we must learn regarding how to

Martin Luther has often been attributed with saying, "You cannot keep birds from flying over your head, but you can keep them from building a nest in your hair."

It is good for us to be without vices, but it is not good for us to be without temptations. Why?

Without temptations, we do not need God and will not be drawn into the riches of his love for us. When our Father leads us into temptation, he calls us into battle, shows us our desperate need for his Son, and empowers us by his Spirit to run to Christ to save us. In him alone will we find the grace and mercy to overcome our temptations and be delivered from evil.[32]

Step Six: Answer the Review Questions with Answer Key

Try to answer the Review Questions below on your own before you refer to the Answer Key in the back of the book.

1. What does James mean when he wrote that God himself tempts no one?[i]

---

overcome temptation: (1) *Starve it out*: We must learn to starve our sinful nature of those things which nourish and feed it. Paul writes, "Make no provision for the flesh, to gratify its desires" (Rom. 13:14). (2) *Cut it out*: We must learn to take radical action against indwelling sin. Jesus teaches: "If your right eye causes you to sin, tear it out and throw it away" (Matt. 5:27–30). The Puritans called this our "mortification" of sin. (3) *Crowd it out*: We must learn to crowd out temptations by replacing them with things that are true, good, and beautiful. After Paul says, "Flee youthful passions," he adds, "And pursue righteousness, faith, love, and peace" (2 Tim. 2:22). A well-cultivated, flourishing garden has much less room for weeds. The Puritans called this our "vivification" in holiness.

32. Augustine writes: "When we say, deliver us from evil, there remains nothing further which ought to be asked. When we have once asked for God's protection against evil, and have obtained it, then against everything which the devil and the world work against us, we stand secure and safe. For what fear is there in this life, to the man whose guardian in this life is God?" Quoted in Calvin, *Sermon on the Mount*, 36–37.

2. What are the three major sources of evil that are the enemy of your soul?[ii]
3. What are the two invaluable promises in Scripture to help us overcome temptation?[iii]

Step Seven: Answer the Discussion Questions with Sample Answers

Reflect on these questions either individually or in a group. They are intended to renew your understanding, stir your heart's desires, and deepen your love for God and others. Try to answer each question on your own before consulting the sample answers in the Answer Key.

1. Mind for Truth: If temptations are often necessary, why ask God not to lead you into them?[iv]
2. Heart for God: What personal vulnerability makes you most aware of your need for the Lord's protection?[v]
3. Life for Ministry: How would you encourage others who are praying this petition, yet seem to be overcome by many temptations?[vi]

Step Eight: Take the Review Quiz with Answer Key

This quiz is designed to help you recall and apply key concepts you're learning, increasing your understanding of these concepts for practical application in life and ministry. Try to answer each question on your own before you refer to the Answer Key.

1. Does God lead us into temptations? (Choose all that apply.)
   a. Yes, in the sense that he allows us to be tested.

b. Yes, in the sense that he wants to know whether we would fail.

c. No, in the sense that he never entices us to sin.

d. No, in the sense that he never allows any harm to come to his children.

2. Why should we ask God to spare us these temptations if they are necessary for us to grow and flourish spiritually?

a. because we know how weak we are and how easy it is for us to fail God's test

b. because we should avoid all kinds of temptations in any possible way

c. because we should prioritize God's protection over our growth

d. none of the above

3. What are the three sources of evil that are the enemy of our soul?

a. the world, the flesh, the desires

b. the devil, the lust, the world

c. the flesh, the world, the devil

d. the greed, the anger, the pride

4. What are the two strategies of Satan's attack to entice us to sin?

a. the outward attack by use of the world and the inward attack by use of our human nature (flesh)

b. the need for our significance and our security

c. the attack on our pride and the hurt on our ego

d. the appeal to our anger and to our greed

. . .

5. What promise or promises did God give to help us overcome temptation? (Choose all that apply.)

a. He will not let us be tempted beyond our ability.

b. He will not lead us to temptations at all costs because of what Jesus has done.

c. He will provide the way of escape so that we may endure.

d. He will provide tremendous reward when we overcome our temptations.

6. "It is good for us to be without vices, but it is not good for us to be without temptations."[vii]

a. true

b. false

Answer Key

Chapter 6 quiz answers are found in the Answer Key.[viii]

Step Nine: Meditate and Pray

All theology should lead us to doxology. The ultimate goal of learning biblical and theological truths is not just to renew our minds, but also to renew our heart affections so that our lives are renewed to the honor of God. Pause now to meditate on and pray about what God is teaching you in his Word. After you pray, consider recording any new insights for application later. Use this prayer outline below if you find it helpful.

- Praise God for giving you his sure promises to help you overcome temptation.
- Confess your weakness in falling prey to the world, the flesh, and the devil.

- Thank Jesus for his faithfulness in overcoming the temptations of the cross so that you will not suffer God's wrath.
- Ask the Holy Spirit to give you faith and strength to endure temptation and always draw near to God for help when it is needed.

Here is an example of how you can pray through the petition, "Lead us not into temptation but deliver us from evil" in the Lord's Prayer. You can use this as a guide during personal devotions, with your family, in small groups, or with your congregation.

Our Father in heaven, we recognize that life is a spiritual battle that is full of trials and temptations that we cannot overcome by our own strength. We ask you to guard us and protect us. Do not lead us into situations that would overwhelm us or cause us to fall. Instead, strengthen us so that we will stand firm against and flee from whatever would draw us away from you, knowing that you never tempt us to evil, but that you often allow trials for our growth. Deliver us from the evil one, who seeks to destroy us and lead us away from you and your good and perfect will for our lives. Protect us from the schemes of Satan this day, especially as he works through the sinful desires of our own hearts and the lure of the world's false promises. Remind us how Christ has overcome Satan, the lure of the world and the flesh for us. Help us to draw near to him in repentance and faith so that we can experience his victory over all forms of evil.

Step Ten: Go Deeper as a Lifelong Learner

This step encourages your deeper exploration by using key resources drawn from the chapter article and academic notes to help you grow in your understanding and application of biblical truths, promoting your lifelong learning and continued growth in spiritual maturity.

BIBLE PASSAGES

Gain a deeper understanding and application of the key biblical passages from the chapter article through more in-depth reading, reflection, study, memorization, and meditation.

> "Then Jesus was led up by the Spirit into the wilderness to be tempted by the devil. And after fasting forty days and forty nights, he was hungry. And the tempter came and said to him, 'If you are the Son of God, command these stones to become loaves of bread.' But he answered, 'It is written, "Man shall not live by bread alone, but by every word that comes from the mouth of God."' Then the devil took him to the holy city and set him on the pinnacle of the temple and said to him, 'If you are the Son of God, throw yourself down, for it is written, "He will command his angels concerning you," and "On their hands they will bear you up, lest you strike your foot against a stone."' Jesus said to him, 'Again it is written, "You shall not put the Lord your God to the test."' Again, the devil took him to a very high mountain and showed him all the kingdoms of the world and their glory. And he said to him, 'All these I will give you, if you will fall down and worship me.' Then Jesus said to him, 'Be gone, Satan! For it is written, "You shall worship the Lord your God and him only shall you serve."'

Then the devil left him, and behold, angels came and were ministering to him." (Matt. 4:1–11)

"When the devil had ended every temptation, he departed from him [Jesus] until an opportune time." (Luke 4:13)

"Hear then the parable of the sower:

When anyone hears the word of the kingdom and does not understand it, the evil one comes and snatches away what has been sown in his heart. This is what was sown along the path.

As for what was sown on rocky ground, this is the one who hears the word and immediately receives it with joy, yet he has no root in himself, but endures for a while, and when tribulation or persecution arises on account of the word, immediately he falls away.

As for what was sown among thorns, this is the one who hears the word, but the cares of the world and the deceitfulness of riches choke the word, and it proves unfruitful.

As for what was sown on good soil, this is the one who hears the word and understands it. He indeed bears fruit and yields, in one case a hundredfold, in another sixty, and in another thirty." (Matt. 13:18–23)

"For from within, out of the heart of man, come evil thoughts, sexual immorality, theft, murder, adultery, coveting, wickedness, deceit, sensuality, envy, slander, pride, foolishness. All these evil things come from within, and they defile a person." (Mark 7:21–23)

"'My Father, if it be possible, let this cup pass from me; nevertheless, not as I will, but as you will.' . . . 'Watch and pray that you may not enter into temptation. The spirit indeed is willing, but the flesh is weak.'" (Matt. 26:39, 41)

"And you were dead in the trespasses and sins in which you once walked, following the course of this world, following the prince of the power of the air, the spirit that is now at work in the sons of disobedience—among whom we all once lived in the passions of our flesh, carrying out the desires of the body and the mind, and were by nature children of wrath, like the rest of mankind." (Eph. 2:1–3)

"Finally, be strong in the Lord and in the strength of his might. Put on the whole armor of God, that you may be able to stand against the schemes of the devil. . . . Therefore take up the whole armor of God, that you may be able to withstand in the evil day, and having done all, to stand firm. Stand therefore, having fastened on the belt of truth, and having put on the breastplate of righteousness, . . . praying at all times in the Spirit, with all prayer and supplication." (Eph. 6:10–18)

"No temptation has overtaken you that is not common to man. God is faithful, and he will not let you be tempted beyond your ability, but with the temptation he will also provide the way of escape, that you may be able to endure it." (1 Cor. 10:13)

"For we do not have a high priest who is unable to sympathize with our weaknesses, but one who in every respect has been tempted as we are, yet without sin. Let us then with confidence draw near to the throne of grace, that we may receive mercy and find grace to help in time of need." (Heb. 4:15–16)

"[Look] to Jesus, the founder and perfecter of our faith, who for the joy that was set before him endured the cross, despising the shame, and is seated at the right hand of the throne of God." (Heb. 12:2)

"Beloved, do not be surprised at the fiery trial when it comes upon you to test you, as though something strange were happening to you. But rejoice insofar as you share Christ's sufferings, that you may also rejoice and be glad when his glory is revealed." (I Peter 4:12–13)

"Humble yourselves, therefore, under the mighty hand of God so that at the proper time he may exalt you, casting all your anxieties on him, because he cares for you. Be sober-minded; be watchful. Your adversary the devil prowls around like a roaring lion, seeking someone to devour. Resist him, firm in your faith, knowing that the same kinds of suffering are being experienced by your brotherhood throughout the world. And after you have suffered a little while, the God of all grace, who has called you to his eternal glory in Christ, will himself restore, confirm, strengthen, and establish you. To him be the dominion forever and ever. Amen." (I Peter 5:6–11)

"Count it all joy, my brothers, when you meet trials of various kinds, for you know that the testing of your faith produces steadfastness. And let steadfastness have its full effect, that you may be perfect and complete, lacking in nothing." (James 1:2–4)

"Blessed is the man who remains steadfast under trial, for when he has stood the test he will receive the crown of life, which God has promised to those who love him. Let no one say when he is tempted, 'I am being tempted by God,' for God cannot be tempted with evil, and he himself tempts no one. But each person is tempted when he is lured and enticed by his own desire." (James 1:12–14)

"'God opposes the proud but gives grace to the humble.' Submit yourselves therefore to God. Resist the devil, and he will flee from you. Draw near to God, and he will draw near to you." (James 4:6–8)

CATECHISMS

Explore key biblical truths through historic Christian catechisms that offer clear guidance on their meaning and life application.

Westminster Shorter Catechism (Q. 106)

- Q. 106: What do we pray for in the sixth petition?
- A. In the sixth petition, which is, *And lead us not into temptation, but deliver us from evil*, we pray that God would either keep us from being tempted to sin, or support and deliver us when we are tempted.

Westminster Larger Catechism (Q. 195)

- Q. 195: What do we pray for in the sixth petition?
- A. In the sixth petition (which is, *And lead us not into temptation, but deliver us from evil*), acknowledging that the most wise, righteous, and gracious God, for divers holy and just ends, may so order things, that we may be assaulted, foiled, and for a time led captive by temptations; that Satan, the world, and the flesh, are ready powerfully to draw us aside, and ensnare us; and that we, even after the pardon of our sins, by reason of our corruption, weakness, and want of watchfulness, are not only subject to be tempted, and forward to expose ourselves unto temptations, but also of ourselves unable and unwilling to resist them, to recover out of them, and

to improve them; and worthy to be left under the power of them; we pray, that God would so overrule the world and all in it, subdue the flesh, and restrain Satan, order all things, bestow and bless all means of grace, and quicken us to watchfulness in the use of them, that we and all his people may by his providence be kept from being tempted to sin; or, if tempted, that by his Spirit we may be powerfully supported and enabled to stand in the hour of temptation; or when fallen, raised again and recovered out of it, and have a sanctified use and improvement thereof: that our sanctification and salvation may be perfected, Satan trodden under our feet, and we fully freed from sin, temptation, and all evil, forever.

Heidelberg Catechism (Q. 127)

- Q. 127: What does the sixth petition mean?
- A. "And do not bring us to the time of trial, but rescue us from the evil one" means: By ourselves we are too weak to hold our own even for a moment. And our sworn enemies—the devil, the world, and our own flesh—never stop attacking us. And so, Lord, uphold us and make us strong with the strength of your Holy Spirit, so that we may not go down to defeat in this spiritual struggle, but may firmly resist our enemies until we finally win the complete victory.

BOOKS

Expand your understanding of key biblical concepts

through selected books that offer more in-depth exploration and practical application.

- Thomas Brooks, *Precious Remedies Against Satan's Devices*—Brooks exposes the devil's tactics to lead believers into sin, pairing each with practical, Scripture-based remedies. This Puritan classic provides valuable insights for resisting temptation and overcoming spiritual challenges.

- C.S. Lewis, *The Screwtape Letters*—Through fictional letters from a senior demon to his apprentice, Lewis explores the nature of temptation and the subtle ways that the devil tries to lead believers astray. This work offers profound insights into spiritual warfare and the Christian's daily struggle against evil.

- John Bunyan, *The Pilgrim's Progress*—This classic allegory follows Christian's journey from the City of Destruction to the Celestial City (heaven). Through trials and encounters with characters such as Faithful, Hopeful, and the giant Despair, Bunyan explores faith, perseverance, and reliance on God in the face of temptations and trials.

HYMNS

Allow these biblical truths to lead you to praise and worship God with prayers and hymns that honor God for who he is and what he does.

- "Come, Thou Fount of Every Blessing," by Robert Robinson—This classic hymn acknowledges our tendency to wander and expresses a heartfelt plea for God to take our hearts and secure them to himself for his heavenly courts above.

- "How Firm a Foundation," by John Rippon—This beloved hymn offers profound assurance of God's promises when facing trials, encouraging believers to stand strong, relying on God's unchanging love and grace.

- "A Mighty Fortress Is Our God," by Martin Luther— Declaring God as a strong protector, this hymn reminds believers of the almighty power of God against the forces of evil, echoing the assurance found in Ephesians 6 to "stand firm" in spiritual warfare.

CONCLUSION: YOUR NEXT STEPS

T he traditional ending of the Lord's Prayer includes the doxology, "For yours is the kingdom and the power and the glory, forever. Amen" (Matt. 6:13 ESV footnote). It's not included in many modern Bible translations because it's not in the earliest Greek manuscripts of the New Testament.[1]

Church leaders probably added this doxology as a benediction to the end of the Lord's Prayer as a part of a public worship liturgy.[2] It seems to be based on King David's temple prayer in 1 Chronicles 29:11–13:

---

1. The traditional doxology is found in the majority of New Testament Greek manuscripts (Textus Receptus and Majority Text), including the Greek uncials dating from the fifth through tenth centuries and the Greek minuscules dating from the ninth through twelfth centuries. This is why the doxology is included in the English KJV and NKJV translations. But the doxology is not found in the earlier and best Greek manuscripts, including א, B, D, fı, various Latin and Coptic versions, and numerous church fathers. It's also not found in Luke's account of the Lord's Prayer in Luke 11:2–4. So most modern English Bible translations do not include it or it's placed in a margin or footnote, e.g., RSV and NIV.

2. It is fine for believers to use this doxology to conclude the prayer, but it should not be seen as belonging to Jesus' teaching.

Yours, O LORD, is the greatness and the power and the glory and the victory and the majesty, for all that is in the heavens and in the earth is yours. Yours is the kingdom, O LORD, and you are exalted as head above all. Both riches and honor come from you, and you rule over all. In your hand are power and might, and in your hand it is to make great and to give strength to all. And now we thank you, our God, and praise your glorious name.

David shows the God-centered nature of his temple prayer by his repeated use of the second-person pronouns *yours* and *you*. David repeatedly prays phrases such as: "*Yours*, O LORD, is the greatness and the power and the glory and the victory and the majesty. . . . *Yours* is the kingdom, O LORD, and *you* are exalted" (1 Chron. 29:11). We see echoes of David's prayer in the benediction, "For *yours* is the kingdom and the power and the glory, forever. Amen."

THIS CONCLUSION PROVIDES your final learning path which includes seven steps. The first two steps focus on concluding your study of the prayer, with an emphasis on the doxology:

- **Step One:** Answer the Review Question with the Answer Key
- **Step Two:** Meditate on and Pray the Doxology

The next three steps guide you in wrapping up your entire study of the prayer, offering a comprehensive review:

- **Step Three:** Take the Cumulative Quiz
- **Step Four:** Read the Book Summary
- **Step Five:** Review the Book Milestones

Finally, the last two steps encourage you to set aside dedicated time to pray through all the petitions, making this the practical culmination of your study:

- **Step Six:** Reflect on Each Petition
- **Step Seven:** Pray All the Petitions

Step One: Answer the Review Question with Answer Key

Try to answer the Review Question below on your own before you refer to the Answer Key.

- Do you pray the Lord's Prayer doxology, knowing that it was likely added later? Why?[i]

Step Two: Meditate on and Pray the Doxology

Here is an example of how you can pray through the doxology in the Lord's Prayer. You can use this as a guide during personal devotions, with your family, in small groups, or with your congregation.

> *Our Father in heaven, your kingdom is forever. You reign over all creation, and we ask that your kingdom continue to expand in our hearts and throughout the world. Conquer our rebellious hearts. Help us live faithfully and joyfully under your rule, longing for the day when your kingdom will come in fullness and every knee will bow before you. In the meantime, use us as your instruments to proclaim the good news of your reign and to seek your will in all we do.*

*Yours is the power and the glory forever. We
rely on the power of your Holy Spirit to protect
and sustain us. We pray that all honor and
praise would be given to you—Father, Son, and
Holy Spirit—for who you are and for your
mighty works of creation, redemption, and
restoration of all things. May our lives reflect
your glory as we eagerly await the day when
your glory fills the earth and all nations
worship you forever.*

Step Three: Take the Cummulative Quiz

1. What is the ultimate focus of the first three petitions of the
Lord's Prayer?
   a. God's honor
   b. human needs
   c. God's will
   d. God's kingdom

2. What is our life purpose revealed in the Lord's Prayer?
   a. to depend on the Lord for all things we need
   b. to defeat the powers of darkness and spiritual authority
   c. to hallow the Father's name by causing his kingdom to
come and will to be done
   d. to seek for eternal goods and not temporal goods

3. Why does Jesus instruct his disciples to pray by using plural
pronouns such as *our, us,* and *we*?
   a. to protect them from addressing God as "My Father"
   b. to discourage them from praying for their personal needs
   c. to emphasize the communal nature of the Christian faith

d. to remind them of the presence of the Holy Spirit during their prayers

4. What is God's ultimate purpose for all things?
    a. that they would be fruitful and multiply
    b. that they would display the honor and glory of his name
    c. that they would live in fullness now
    d. that they would pass away to reveal his permanent glory

5. When will believers experience the ability to perfectly obey God's will?
    a. upon their conversion
    b. near the end of their earthly sanctification
    c. never
    d. when they are in resurrected bodies

6. What are we asking when we pray for the Father's will to be done on earth as it is in heaven?
    a. for God to change his decretive will
    b. for God to complete his preceptive will
    c. for God to align our hearts with his revealed will
    d. for God to accomplish his mysterious will among us

7. What is the superior gift in praying for our "daily bread"? (Choose all that apply.)
    a. the things that we ask for
    b. the gift of God in the Holy Spirit
    c. the things that we never knew we needed
    d. the food that we eat every day

· · ·

8. Why did our heavenly Father not always give Jesus the daily physical care and comfort he desired and requested? (Choose all that apply.)

    a. He knew that Jesus did not need it to carry out his will.

    b. He knew that it was better for Jesus not to have his physical needs met.

    c. He wanted Jesus to experience suffering.

9. Why does Jesus teach us to keep asking our Father to forgive us our sins even when we have already repented and believed in Jesus Christ?

    a. because we keep phasing in and out of God's love and forgiveness

    b. because we should not die with some measure of unconfessed sin

    c. because those who are forgiven show it by drawing near to God in repentance and faith

    d. because we need to keep up our "good works" so that God will keep forgiving us

10. When you forgive someone, you _____. (Choose all that apply.)

    a. rationalize and minimize the person's sins

    b. reveal that you have been forgiven

    c. follow Jesus, who paid your debt that you could not pay

    d. phase into God's love and forgiveness

11. Why should we ask God to spare us these temptations if they are necessary for us to grow and flourish spiritually?

    a. because we know how weak we are and how easy it is for us to fail God's test

b. because we should avoid all kinds of temptations in any possible way

c. because we should prioritize God's protection over our growth

d. none of the above

12. What promise or promises did God give to help us overcome temptation? (Choose all that apply.)

a. He will not let us be tempted beyond our ability.

b. He will not lead us to temptations at all costs because of what Jesus has done.

c. He will provide the way of escape so that we may endure.

d. He will provide tremendous reward when we overcome our temptations.

Answer Key

Answers to the Next Steps Cumulative Quiz are found in the Answer Key.[ii]

Step Four: Review the Book Summary

In this book, you learned how to develop a strong hope rooted in the rich biblical truths found in the Lord's Prayer. You were equipped to:

- understand the setting, meaning, and purpose of the Lord's Prayer.
- learn how to ask our Father in heaven to honor his name.
- pray for God's kingdom and will to come on earth as it is in heaven.

- petition God for our daily needs, protection, and obedience in faith.
- ask God to forgive our sins as we forgive those who sin against us.
- request God not to lead us into temptation but deliver us from evil.

Step Five: Review the Key Milestones

These milestones are measurable outcomes designed to help you grow in your knowledge, character, and skills with others in community, under the oversight of a qualified mentor, coach, or facilitator.

_____ I know the context of the Lord's Prayer and its intended purpose for Jesus' disciples.

_____ I grasp the communal nature of faith reflected in praying to God as our Father and how to pray for God's name to be set apart and honored in prayer.

_____ I understand how to ask God to glorify his name by causing his kingdom to come and for God's will to be done on earth as it is in heaven.

_____ I know how to pray for God's daily provisions for all things we need for life and for our daily protection, trusting in the Father's care.

_____ I know what it means to pray for God's ongoing forgiveness of our sins as we forgive others.

_____ I know why and how I need to ask our Father not to lead us into temptation and what it means to ask our Father to keep delivering us from evil.

Step Six: Reflect on Each Petition

The ultimate goal of the three *horizontal petitions* in the Lord's Prayer (for our daily bread, our forgiveness, and our protection) is to see our Father's answers to the three *vertical petitions* (for his name to be honored, his kingdom to come, and his will to be done on earth as it is in heaven).

Our Father uses our daily needs, sinful failures, and temptations to keep drawing us near to himself so that through his ongoing provisions of our daily bread, forgiveness, and protection, he sweeps us up into his higher purposes for the world to see his name honored, his kingdom come, and his will be done on earth as it is in heaven—through us.

God's primary purpose for creating the world is so that all the nations would glorify, worship, and find their joy in him. This is why we exist—to glorify God by enjoying him and helping to extend the worship and enjoyment of God to all nations.

The Christian hope is that when Jesus returns, he will make all things new so that God the Father will be honored and glorified in everything forever (1 Cor. 15:24–25, 28). In the meantime, Jesus calls us to join with him and pray the Lord's Prayer.

Step Seven: Pray All the Petitions

This learning step compiles all the sample prayers from chapters 2–6, giving you a complete guide to help you pray through the entire Lord's Prayer.

Our Father in heaven, hallowed be your name.

Our Father in heaven, we come before you as our loving Father who cares for us with an everlasting love, and as our sovereign King who reigns over all things from your heavenly throne to carry out your good and perfect will in our lives and in the whole world. We ask you to hallow your name on earth as it is now hallowed in heaven where angels ceaselessly bring praise, honor, and glory to you for the greatness of who you are and for all that you do in your magnificent acts of creation and redemption. Honor your name in and through our lives by deepening our knowledge of you, strengthening our love for you, and increasing our joy and delight in you above all else.

Your kingdom come, your will be done, on earth as it is in heaven.

Our Father in heaven, we ask you to hallow your name by causing your kingdom to come and your will to be done on earth as it is in heaven. Glorify your name by accomplishing your purpose for our fallen and broken world – to redeem and restore all things through your Son, Jesus Christ, by the power of your Holy Spirit. Cause your invisible rule in heaven, where your will is perfectly accomplished, to become more visible on earth and in our lives, so that we and all things may flourish according to your design and give you the honor that you alone deserve for who you are and for all you do. Give us the grace and power to seek first your kingdom and your will in all things with our whole heart.

Give us this day our daily bread.

We come before you, asking for our daily bread, trusting in your perfect provision for all our physical and spiritual needs. Provide us with everything necessary to fulfill your will— whether in abundance or in scarcity—trusting that each day's bread comes from your loving hand. Guard us from the tempta- tion to rely on material security and teach us to depend fully on you, knowing that you care for us in every circumstance. As we ask for our daily bread, grant us contentment with whatever you provide, whether we are in plenty or in want. Remind us that our true sustenance comes from you and your perfect will. In both our need and abundance, strengthen our hearts to trust in your promises. Remind us that you will always give us exactly what we need to honor your name, advance your kingdom, and carry out your will. Grant us grace this day to depend fully on you and to be generous with others, reflecting your love and care in all that we do.

Forgive us our debts, as we also have forgiven our debtors.

We humbly acknowledge that we owe you a debt that we can never repay because of our many sins. Yet, through the perfect life, sacrificial death, and resurrection of Jesus Christ in our place, you have made a way for our immense debt to be forgiven. Cleanse us from all our sins and help us to live in the freedom and joy of knowing that we are fully forgiven and justified in your sight through Jesus' blood and righteousness. As you have forgiven us for our sins, grant us the grace to forgive those who have wronged us. Just as you have mercifully released us from our debts, give us the power to release others from what they owe us. Free our hearts from resentment and bitterness. Teach us to reflect your mercy by forgiving as we have been forgiven. May your forgiveness bring reconciliation and peace, allowing us to reflect to others the abundant mercy that we have received from you.

Lead us not into temptation, but deliver us from evil.

Our Father in heaven, we recognize that life is a spiritual battle that is full of trials and temptations that we cannot overcome by our own strength. We ask you to guard us and protect us. Do not lead us into situations that would overwhelm us or cause us to fall. Instead, strengthen us so that we will stand firm against and flee from whatever would draw us away from you, knowing that you never tempt us to evil, but that you often allow trials for our growth. Deliver us from the evil one, who seeks to destroy us and lead us away from you and your good and perfect will for our lives. Protect us from the schemes of Satan this day, especially as he works through the sinful desires of our own hearts and the lure of the world's false promises. Remind us how Christ has overcome Satan, the lure of the world and the flesh for us. Help us to draw near to him in repentance and faith so that we can experience his victory over all forms of evil.

For yours is the kingdom and the power and the glory, forever.

Our Father in heaven, your kingdom is forever. You reign over all creation, and we ask that your kingdom continue to expand in our hearts and throughout the world. Conquer our rebellious hearts. Help us live faithfully and joyfully under your rule, longing for the day when your kingdom will come in fullness and every knee will bow before you. In the meantime, use us as your instruments to proclaim the good news of your reign and to seek your will in all we do. Yours is the power and the glory forever. We rely on the power of your Holy Spirit to protect and sustain us. We pray that all honor and praise would be given to you—Father, Son, and Holy Spirit—for who you are and for your mighty works of creation, redemption, and the restoration of all things. May our lives reflect your glory as we eagerly await the day when your glory fills the earth and all nations worship you forever.

ANSWER KEY

1. Our Hope

i. **Review Question 1 Answer:** In Matthew, the Lord's Prayer is taught early in Jesus' ministry during the Sermon on the Mount in Galilee, focusing on the importance of sincere prayer to our Father amidst warnings against hypocrisy. In Luke, the prayer is taught later in Jesus' ministry in Judea, in response to a disciple's request. The emphasis in this context is on persistence and boldness in prayer when seeking God's purposes.

ii. **Review Question 2 Answer:** The Lord's Prayer is divided into two sections: Godward petitions which focus on God's honor, and manward petitions focused on human needs. They must be seen as a cohesive whole with the manward petitions understood as asking for the means necessary to fulfill the Godward petitions.

iii. **Review Question 3 Answer:** We should use the Lord's Prayer as a model for all of our prayers. Our prayers (and our lives) should be rooted in the framework of the Lord's Prayer. Whether using the exact words or not, our prayers should reflect the reality that our life's mission is the same as Jesus', to glorify the Father's name in the coming of his kingdom and the doing of his will. When we pray for our needs of daily bread, forgiveness, and deliverance from evil, we should trust God to provide for us so that we will glorify his name by advancing his kingdom and accomplishing his will.

iv. **Review Question 4 Answer:** The ultimate purpose of the Lord's Prayer is to align my life with God's purposes by glorifying his name, seeking the advancement of his kingdom, and submitting to his will. The prayer teaches me that my daily physical needs, my forgiveness, and my deliverance from evil are all necessary for me to live out this mission.

v. **Discussion Question 1 Sample Answer:** The priorities of the Lord's Prayer are often absent from the priorities of prayers, especially a focus on God's glory and the coming of his kingdom and the doing of his will. The Lord's Prayer has been recited without meaning and is sometimes used as almost a lucky charm or superstition by sports teams and at business meetings.

vi. **Discussion Question 2 Sample Answer:** My life and prayers are less centered on God himself than the focus in the Lord's Prayer. Focusing first on his name, his kingdom, and his will reminds me that my life is about his honor, kingdom, and will. Addressing God as my loving Father should deepen my trust in him and remind me that my needs are important, but only as they relate to his greater purposes. When I ask for daily bread, forgiveness, and protection, I remember that it is not just about me; it's about aligning my life with God's purposes.

vii. **Discussion Question 3 Sample Answer:** Praying the Lord's Prayer regularly helps me grow in my love for God by constantly reorienting my priorities around his glory, kingdom and will. It also challenges me to love others, especially when I pray for forgiveness "as we also have forgiven our debtors." This connection between receiving and giving forgiveness motivates me to practice grace in my relationships. Additionally, the communal aspect of the prayer—using "our" instead of "my"—reminds me that I'm part of a larger body of believers, encouraging me to support and care for others in my family, church, and network in their spiritual journeys.

viii. **Chapter 1 Quiz Answers:** (1) b; (2) d; (3) b; (4) a; (5) a; (6) c.

2. Our Father's Name

i. **Review Question 1 Answer:** The phrase "our Father" should deepen my understanding of the communal nature of the Christian faith. It emphasizes that being a follower of Jesus is not just an individual journey but a shared experience with the family of God. It also highlights my adoption into God's family through Christ, giving me the assurance of God's love and care as my Father.

ii. **Review Question 2 Answer:** The phrase "in heaven" reminds me of God's transcendence and sovereignty. It balances the intimacy of calling God "Father" with a reverence for his majesty as the sovereign King in heaven ruling over all creation. This understanding encourages me to approach God with both boldness and humility in prayer, recognizing his power and authority while also trusting in his fatherly love.

iii. **Review Question 3 Answer:** The phrase "hallowed be Your name" shapes my prayer by reminding me that God's name—and by extension, his character—is set apart and should be honored above all else. This focus on God's glory shifts my perspective from self-centered desires to seeking that God's will and holiness be acknowledged and revered in all aspects of my life. It teaches me humility and gives me a God-centered attitude in prayer, prioritizing God's purposes over my personal concerns.

iv. **Review Question 4 Answer:** God's primary purpose for creating the world and humanity is to glorify himself. Everything exists to display the honor and glory of God's name. This includes God's work in creation, redemption, and restoration, all aimed at bringing glory to his name as people and nations come to know and worship him for who he is and what he does.

v. **Discussion Question 1 Sample Answer:** Addressing God as *Father* in the Lord's Prayer deepens my understanding of God as both intimate and personal. It reminds me that through Christ, I am not just a follower and forgiven law-breaker, but an adopted child of God. This shifts my perception from seeing God only as a distant Creator or Judge to recognizing him as a loving Father who cares for me deeply and personally. It shapes my relationship with him as one rooted in love, security, and belonging within his family.

vi. **Discussion Question 2 Sample Answer:** My relationship with God as my Father changes my prayers from being mere formalities or obligations to heartfelt conversations with a loving parent. Knowing God as Father encourages me to pray with confidence and trust, knowing that he desires to hear from me and respond with what is best for me. It also makes my prayers more communal, as I recognize my shared connection with other believers, praying not just for myself but for brothers and sisters in Christ.

vii. **Discussion Question 3 Sample Answer:** Understanding God's zeal for his name to be honored compels me to live in a way that reflects his glory. It motivates me to align my life with his purposes, seeking to honor him in all that I do. This means making choices that prioritize honoring his name, advancing his kingdom, showing integrity in my actions, and sharing the gospel with others. It also motivates me to resist anything that would profane God's name, leading me to live in holiness and to encourage others to do the same.

viii. **Chapter 2 Quiz Answers:** (1) c; (2) a; (3) d; (4) e; (5) a; (6) b.

3. Our Father's Kingdom and Will

i. **Review Question 1 Answer:** The Jews expected the arrival of a Messiah who would deliver them from Roman oppression and establish a powerful earthly kingdom, restoring Israel's glory. Yet Jesus proclaimed a much more comprehensive deliverance from all powers of evil, including the world, sin, the devil, and death. His kingdom extends beyond earthly Israel to a redeemed people from all nations who are saved out of their rebellion and reconciled to God to live forever in a restored creation under God's rule.

ii. **Review Question 2 Answer:** The Father establishes his will in creation. The Son accomplishes the Father's will in his redemption of fallen humanity and the world. The Spirit applies the Son's work of redemption to fallen humanity and the world, thereby restoring the Father's will for his name to be honored, his kingdom to come, and his will to be done on earth as it is in heaven.

iii. **Review Question 3 Answer:** Resurrected believers will differ from Adam and Eve's pre-fall condition in that they will be in a state unlike Adam and Eve, who were "able not to sin" but still "able to sin." While Adam and Eve were created sinless, they were still in a provisional state, subject to the possibility of sin. In contrast, resurrected believers in the world to come will experience a glorious state of not even being able to sin, enjoying perfect obedience to God's will forever.

iv. **Review Question 4 Answer:** God's decretive will is his sovereign, unchangeable plan for everything that happens in my life and in the world. His preceptive will is his revealed moral instruction in Scripture, guiding me in how to live righteously so that I'll flourish in the world according to his good and perfect will. While God's decretive will is hidden, mysterious, and infallible, his preceptive will directs my actions according to his Word.

v. **Discussion Question 1 Sample Answer:** When I pray for God's kingdom to come, I am asking him to hallow his name by making his invisible rule more visible in everything, including his loving rule over all areas of my daily life. I'm asking for his ruling presence to shape my interactions and decisions at work and home. By asking for his will to be done, I'm resolving to obey his will in all my choices, such as being honest in a tough situation that hurts. This alignment with God's kingdom and will empowers me to honor his name and glorify him in practical, everyday ways.

vi. **Discussion Question 2 Sample Answer:** My desire for comfort and control can hinder me from fully trusting in God's plan for my life. This can lead me to cling to my own plans and resist stepping out in faith. To better align my thoughts, desires, and behaviors with God's will, I need to let go of my inordinate desire for certainty and see uncertainties as opportunities—gifts from God—to grow closer to him and trust his guidance in every area of my life.

vii. **Discussion Question 3 Sample Answer:** I can pray for my community by asking God to cultivate a spirit of unity, compassion, and service among us, reflecting the perfect love and obedience seen in heaven. Specifically, I can pray for our local leaders to prioritize initiatives that embody Christ's humility, his generosity, and the common good, reaching out to those in need and living out the values of the kingdom. I can ask God to guide us to be a beacon of hope and reconciliation, actively working to bridge divides and foster a spirit of genuine love and respect among neighbors.

viii. **Chapter 3 Quiz Answers:** (1) a; (2) a; (3) d; (4) b; (5) c; (6) b.

4. Our Daily Bread

i. **Review Question 1 Answer:** Jesus' broader purpose is to cultivate in us a deeper dependence on God for our daily needs, both physical and spiritual. By instructing us to pray for our daily bread, Jesus reminds us of our constant reliance on God's provision, and he calls us to align our requests with his will. This teaches us that our greatest need is not just physical sustenance but a relationship with God, who provides everything necessary for us to fulfill our mission of honoring him, advancing his kingdom, and doing his will.

ii. **Review Question 2 Answer:** Jesus' teaching on persistence in prayer shows me that asking for my daily bread should be a regular practice. It means that I should keep asking and trusting God to provide my daily needs, knowing that his answers are always right and timely, even if they don't match my daily desires.

iii. **Review Question 3 Answer:** I need protection from the temptations of both poverty and riches. Poverty can lead to despair and dishonesty, while wealth can foster self-sufficiency and my lack of need for God. Both temptations pose risks of diverting me from God's mission for my life. By asking for daily bread, I seek God's help for me and others to navigate these temptations and maintain my focus on him and his will.

iv. **Review Question 4 Answer:** I do not always receive what I think is necessary because God's understanding of my needs sometimes differs from mine. His provision is not limited to what I desire but is always aligned with what is truly best for me and for fulfilling his will in and through my life. Not receiving what I ask for leads me to greater dependence on God and helps me grow in faith and obedience, teaching me that his wisdom surpasses my understanding of what I truly need.

v. **Discussion Question 1 Sample Answer:** The petition for daily bread focuses on my greatest need to trust in God rather than trust in my own resources and my own understanding of my needs. It guards me against the temptations that come with having little, such as my struggle with envy and my lack of generosity, and the temptations that come with having much, like my tendency to be arrogantly self-reliant.

vi. **Discussion Question 2 Sample Answer:** I can be tempted to lean on my own understanding regarding financial concerns, especially as I try to plan for unexpected expenses. When I pray for my daily bread, I'm reminded that God is my ultimate provider. This prayer shifts my focus from viewing my needs as mere transactions to seeing them as opportunities to trust in God's faithfulness. I realize that his provision is not just sufficient but also tailored to what is best for me. Each time I acknowledge my reliance on God, I feel a growing sense of peace and assurance that he knows my needs intimately and will care for me.

vii. **Discussion Question 3 Sample Answer:** The regular act of praying this petition reinforces my commitment to God's mission, encouraging me to prioritize his will over my own desires. This shift cultivates gratitude and contentment in my heart, making me more aware of the blessings around me. As I seek God's provision, I also become more open to his guidance, leading me to make decisions that reflect his perfect will, such as offering support to someone in need rather than focusing solely on my own plans.

viii. **Chapter 4 Quiz Answers:** (1) a; (2) b; (3) d; (4) c; (5) a, b; (6) a.

5. Our Forgiveness

i. **Review Question 1 Answer:** My debt to God is my failure to love him and others perfectly, as required by his law. This debt stems from my sin—whether through actions I commit (commission) or things I neglect to do (omission)—which reflects my failure to fully obey his commandments and leaves me morally indebted to him.

ii. **Review Question 2 Answer:** God forgives my debts through Jesus Christ, who lived a sinless life, died in the place of sinners, and was raised from the dead, fully satisfying God's justice on my behalf. Through faith in Christ, my sins are forgiven because he paid the debt that I could never pay. God treated Jesus like a sinner so that he could treat me like Jesus.

iii. **Review Question 3 Answer:** Justified believers continue to confess their sins to restore their broken fellowship with God, even though their salvation is secure. Ongoing repentance and confession help prevent sin from disrupting spiritual growth and deepening communion with God.

iv. **Review Question 4 Answer:** Jesus teaches me to forgive others as a reflection of God's forgiveness toward me. My forgiveness of others is evidence that I have been forgiven by God and transformed by his mercy.

v. **Discussion Question 1 Sample Answer:** Forgiveness does not require me to forget about how I've been sinned against because that can minimize or excuse the sin committed against me. Instead, forgiveness is me making a conscious choice to release the person who sinned against me from the debt that he or she owes me, imitating what God has done for me in Jesus Christ. This acknowledges the wrong against me and helps set me free from the burden of expecting repayment from my offender.

vi. **Discussion Question 2 Sample Answer:** Through my ongoing repentance from sin and faith in Christ, I am reminded of my continual need for God's grace and power. This deepens my dependence on God, strengthens my relationship with him, and redirects my heart from self-reliance to resting in him and his loving mercy for me in Jesus Christ.

vii. **Discussion Question 3 Sample Answer:** God's forgiveness of my sin enables me to forgive others, recognizing that I have been forgiven far more than I can ever forgive. This frees me to treat those who wrong me with grace and mercy, reflecting the same grace and mercy that God consistently extends to me.

viii. **Chapter 5 Quiz Answers:** (1) a, b, c, d, e (2) b (3) a (4) c (5) a (6) b, c

6. Our Protection

i. **Review Question 1 Answer:** James means that God never leads anyone into sin. "Tempt" here refers to drawing someone toward disobedience. While God may allow trials or tests, his goal is to help believers grow in faith, not to make them sin. The urge to sin originates from our sinful desires, not from God.

ii. **Review Question 2 Answer:**
   The World: Ungodly societal beliefs, values, and behaviors that Satan uses to tempt me into disobedience.
   The Flesh: My sinful human nature, which includes desires such as lust, greed, and pride.
   The Devil: Satan, the Evil One, is the primary instigator of evil. He actively entices me into sin through outward attacks (using the world) and inward attacks (through my sinful nature).

iii. **Review Question 3 Answer:**
   God will not tempt you beyond what you can handle: 1 Corinthians 10:13 assures you that God is faithful and will not allow you to be tempted beyond your ability to resist. He knows your limits and always provides the strength you need to endure.

God will provide a way of escape: In 1 Corinthians 10:13, Paul also promises that God will provide a way of escape so that you can endure temptation. This means that God will always provide a means for you to resist temptation and not fall into sin.

iv. **Discussion Question 1 Sample Answer:** I ask God not to lead me into temptation because I know my weakness and vulnerability to sin. While temptations can lead to growth, I pray to avoid them, acknowledging the risk of failure. When God wills such trials, I trust his grace to sustain me, seeking his wisdom and strength to remain faithful.

v. **Discussion Question 2 Sample Answer:** Asking God for protection shows my vulnerability by admitting I can't handle spiritual battles alone. It acknowledges my weakness and draws me closer to him, relying on his power rather than my own. This dependence deepens my faith as I experience his grace, strength, and faithfulness in overcoming challenges.

vi. **Discussion Question 3 Sample Answer:** I would encourage others by reminding them that feeling overwhelmed by temptation is normal for all believers. Even Jesus faced temptation. Praying this petition shows their reliance on God. I'd remind them of God's promises of escape (1 Cor. 10:13) and urge them to persevere, trusting in God's grace and power in their weakness.

vii. **Review Quiz Question 6 Explanation:** TRUE—While being without vices is good, temptations are necessary for spiritual growth. They lead us to rely more on God, showing our need for his strength and grace. God uses them to shape us into Christ's image, helping us grow in maturity and trust in his promises, making temptations essential for faith.

viii. **Chapter 6 Quiz Answers:** (1) a, c (2) a (3) c (4) a (5) a, c (6) a

Conclusion: Your Next Steps

i. **Review Question Answer:** I pray the Lord's Prayer doxology because it reinforces biblical themes of God's sovereignty, power, and glory taught by Jesus. It reminds me of God's authority over my daily provision, forgiveness, and trials. It's a meaningful way to end my prayer, expressing trust and worship.

ii. **Answers:** (1) a; (2) c; (3) c; (4) b; (5) d; (6) c; (7) b; (8) a, b; (9) c; (10) b, c; (11) a; (12) a, c.

SELECTED BIBLIOGRAPHY

The Anglican Book of Common Prayer. Reprint, 1662 ed. Oxford University Press, 2005.

The Anglican Catechism. 1662. Reprint, London: Library House of Lords, 1853.

Augustine, *Confessions*. Penguin Random House, 1961.

Augustine. *The Enchiridion on Faith, Hope, and Love*. Translated by J.F. Shaw. E. P. Dutton, 1955.

Augustine. *On Correction and Grace*. Edited by Philip Schaff. Translated by Peter Holmes. In *A Select Library of the Nicene and Post-Nicene Fathers of the Christian Church, First Series*, vol. 5. Christian Literature Publishing Co., 1887.

Bavinck, Herman. *Reformed Dogmatics*. Vol. 2, *God and Creation*. Edited by John Bolt. Translated by John Vriend. Baker Academic, 2004.

Bonar, Horatius. *The Everlasting Righteousness*. Banner of Truth Trust. 1993.

The Book of Common Prayer, and Administration of the Sacraments and Other Rites and Ceremonies of the Church, Together with the Psalter or Psalms of David, According to the Use of the Episcopal Church. Church Publishing Incorporated, 1979.

Bounds, E.M. *The Complete Works of E.M. Bounds on Prayer*. BakerBooks, 2004.

Brooks, Thomas. *Precious Remedies Against Satan's Devices*. Banner of Truth Trust, 2021.

Bunyan, John. *The Pilgrim's Progress*. B&H Publishing Group, 2023.

Burroughs, Jeremiah. *The Rare Jewel of Christian Contentment*. Banner of Truth Trust, 2022.

Calvin, John. *Commentary on the Gospel of Matthew*. Translated by William Pringle. Banner of Truth Trust, 1958.

Calvin, John. *Commentary on the Sermon on the Mount*. Translated by William Pringle. Banner of Truth Trust, 1959.

Calvin, John. *Institutes of the Christian Religion*. Translated by Henry Beveridge. Hendrickson Publishers, 2008.

DeYoung, Kevin. *The Lord's Prayer: Learning from Jesus on What, Why, and How to Pray*. Foundational Tools for Our Faith. Crossway, 2022.

Edwards, Jonathan. *The End for Which God Created the World: Exposition, Analysis, and Philosophical Implications (New Directions in Jonathan Edwards Studies)*. Edited by Walter J. Schultz. Vandenhoeck & Ruprecht, 2020.

Frame, John M. *The Doctrine of the Christian Life*. P&R Publishing, 2008.

Goldsworthy, Graeme. *Gospel and Kingdom: A Christian Interpretation of the Old Testament*. 2nd ed. Paternoster Press, 1994.

Heber, Reginald. "Holy, Holy, Holy! Lord God Almighty." 1826. Tune by John Bacchus Dykes, NICAEA. First published in *A Selection of Psalms and Hymns for the Parish Church of Banbury*, edited by Amelia Heber. Publisher not specified.

Heidelberg Catechism, 1563. Canadian Reformed Theological Seminary. www.heidelberg-catechism.com. Accessed February 2025.

Henry, Matthew. *A Way to Pray: A Biblical Method for Enriching Your Prayer Life*. Edited by O. Palmer Robertson. Banner of Truth Trust, 2020.

Herklots, Rosamond E. "Forgive Our Sins as We Forgive." In *100 Hymns for Today*, 1969 supplement to *Hymns Ancient and Modern*. Oxford University Press, 1969.

Hoekema, Anthony, A. *Created in God's Image*. Eerdmans, 1994.

Hovey, E. Paul, compiler. *The Treasury of Inspirational Anecdotes, Quotations, and Illustrations*. Fleming H. Revell, 1994.

Hull, Eleanor, trans. "Be Thou My Vision." SLANE arrangement, 1912. In *Hymnal of the Church of Ireland*, 3rd ed., 1919.

Jeremias, Joachim. *New Testament Theology: The Proclamation of Jesus.* Translated by John Bowden. Charles Scribner's Sons, 1971.

John of Avila. *Sermons.* Translated by Richard M. H. Smith. Catholic University of America Press, 1987.

Keller, Timothy. *Counterfeit Gods: The Empty Promises of Money, Sex, and Power, and the Only Hope That Matters.* Penguin Books, 2009.

Keller, Timothy. *Prayer: Experiencing Awe and Intimacy with God.* Dutton, 2014.

Keller, Timothy. *The Prodigal God: Recovering the Heart of the Christian Faith.* Dutton, 2008.

Keller, Timothy, and Sam Shammas, eds. *The New City Catechism: 52 Questions and Answers for Our Hearts and Minds.* Crossway, 2012.

Lewis, C.S. *The Screwtape Letters.* Harcourt Brace, 1942.

Lovelace, Richard. *Dynamics of Spiritual Life: An Evangelical Theology of Renewal,* IVP Academic, 1979.

Luther, Martin. *The Book of Concord: The Confessions of the Evangelical Lutheran Church.* Edited by Robert Kolb and Timothy J. Wengert. Translated by Charles Arand, et al. Fortress Press, 2000.

Luther, Martin. *Luther's Works.* Edited by Gustav K. Wiencke. Fortress Press, 1968.

Luther, Martin. *A Simple Way to Pray: The Life and Wisdom of Luther for Today.* Edited by Archie Parrish. Serve International, Inc., 2005.

Miller, Paul. *A Praying Life: Connecting with God in a Distracting World.* Revised edition. NavPress, 2017.

Morris, Leon. *Apostolic Preaching of the Cross.* Eerdmans, 1955.

Morris, Leon. *The Gospel According to Matthew.* Eerdmans, 1992.

Murray, John. *Redemption Accomplished and Applied.* Eerdmans, 2015.

Owen, John. *On Mortification of Sin*, 1656. Reprint, Banner of Truth Trust, 2004.

Packer, J.I. *Growing in Christ*. Crossway, 1994.

Packer, J.I. *Knowing God*. InterVarsity Press, 1993.

Packer, J. I. *Praying the Lord's Prayer*. Crossway, 2007.

Piper, John. *Desiring God: Meditations of a Christian Hedonist*. Multnomah Books, 2011.

Piper, John. *Let the Nations Be Glad!: The Supremacy of God in Missions*. Edited by David Mathis. 3rd edition. Baker Academic, 2010.

Ridderbos, Herman. *The Coming of the Kingdom*. P&R Publishing Company, 1962.

Smith, Walter Chalmers. "Immortal, Invisible, God Only Wise." In *Hymns of Christ and the Christian Life*. Alexander Strahan, 1867.

Sproul, R.C. *The Barber Who Wanted to Pray*. Illustrated by T. Lively Fluharty. Crossway, a division of Good News Publishers. 2011.

Stott, John. *The Cross of Christ*. InterVarsity Press, 1986.

Ursinus, Zacharias, and Caspar Olevianus. The Heidelberg Catechism. Translated by Fred H. Klooster. Baker, 1984.

Watson, Thomas. *All Things for Good: A Puritan Guide*. Bibliotech Press, 2020.

Watson, Thomas. *The Art of Divine Contentment*. Soli Deo Gloria, 2019.

Watson, Thomas. *The Lord's Prayer: A Guide to Praying to Our Father*. Banner of Truth Trust, 1984.

Westminster Assembly. *The Westminster Larger Catechism: Agreed upon by the Assembly of Divines at Westminster, with the Assistance of Commissioners from the Church of Scotland*. 1647.

Westminster Assembly. *The Westminster Shorter Catechism: Agreed upon by the Assembly of Divines at Westminster, with the Assistance of Commissioners from the Church of Scotland*. 1647.

SCRIPTURE INDEX

SUBJECT AND NAMES INDEX

TAKE THE ONLINE COURSE

Renewing Your Hope with the Lord's Prayer by Childers and
Frame is now available as a Pathway Learning online course.

LEARN YOUR WAY
- Study on all your devices
- Learn at your own pace
- Test your progress with instant results
- Earn a free certificate of completion

LEARN TOGETHER
- Form your own online group
- Start anytime (90-day access)
- Invite friends and family to join
- Learn together and track progress

SPECIAL OFFER FOR READERS

Get the full course for 50% off!

- Just visit the following link:

https://courses.pathwaylearning.org/library/renewing-your-hope-course-the-lord-s-prayer-179956/about/

- Then create your free account
- Enter the promo code below:

ONLINEPRAYERCOURSE

ABOUT PATHWAY LEARNING

We partner to help underserved church leaders plant and grow healthy churches that transform lives and communities around the world.

What Problem Do We Want to Help Solve?

Millions of gifted and called church leaders, especially in the non-Western world, do not have access to the high quality, seminary-level training and tools they need to plant and grow healthy churches that have effective ministries of evangelism, discipleship, and mercy. They can't afford to leave their families and churches to learn in a new language and culture.

What Is Our Solution?

In response, we've developed an innovative blend of online and on-site curriculum that provides underserved church leaders with access to affordable, practical seminary-level resources in their language and adapted to their culture. Our courses and books focus not only on developing church leaders' knowledge, but also on the character and practical skills they need to be effective in ministry.

What Is Our Strategy?

We establish strategic kingdom partnerships with church-leader training organizations, such as indigenous denominations, networks, mission agencies, seminaries, and churches, to help *them* be more effective in training *their* church leaders to plant and grow healthy churches. This allows us to leverage our ministry to have the greatest possible impact.

How Can You Partner With Us?

We're looking for new partners to help us bring this solution to more church leaders around the world. There are three ways you can partner with us:

- Become a prayer partner, praying for our ministries around the world.
- Become a giving partner, supporting us financially.
- Become a ministry partner who uses our resources to help equip your church leaders.

Learn more at www.pathwaylearning.org. Email us at hello@pathwaylearning.org.

www.ingramcontent.com/pod-product-compliance
Lightning Source LLC
Chambersburg PA
CBHW060416130626
46555CB00005B/2085